Chasing Life

Gary Hope

"Chasing Life," by Gary Hope. ISBN 978-1-63868-030-7 (softcover).

Published 2021 by Virtualbookworm.com Publishing Inc., P.O. Box 9949, College Station, TX , 77842, US.

THE ONE THING THAT GOLF HAS TAUGHT ME is that no one can learn golf . . . it's impossible. It's like trying to learn Chinese, Swahili, Russian, Greek, and Pig-Latin all at the same time: chipping, putting, driving, long-irons, short-irons; can't be done. I was watching a top professional tournament on television and the guy in second place four-putted from fifteen feet . . . four-putted! These pros hit the ball in the water, sliced it out of bounds, flubbed their chip shots, and cursed relentlessly—and they're the best players on earth. What are we normal humans supposed to do?

The answer, of course, is nothing. Try to enjoy it and learn from what the game has to teach. It's hard to do that. I know, because I've thrown clubs, slammed clubs in the ground, cursed myself, cursed golf, cursed Jerry, and cursed my measly existence, all to no avail. I've heard golf described as "a good walk spoiled." I've seen people bet thousands of dollars on one shot—ONE SHOT! I've seen golfers act like the biggest jerks on the planet. I've seen others cheat on their scores, cheat on their friends, and ultimately cheat themselves out of any joy and fun that could have been available. All in the name of golf. My friend Arthur told me they named it "golf" because all the other four-letter words were taken. I believe him.

My Uncle Paul taught me how to play golf. As a twelve-year-old, I had no clue. I only had five golf clubs and held them as I would hold a baseball bat. Uncle Paul molded me, instructed

1

me, and had the patience to never give up. However, as much as he loved golf and tried to teach me some golf skills, the thing he taught me most was about life. Golf was only the conduit to use for learning. I don't think he intended to teach me anything aside from golf but he couldn't help it. It's the way he was. As you've probably guessed, he's putting and driving and chipping up in heaven now, and all I have left are the memories and life lessons he passed on through his unbelievable patience with a young man who thought he already knew it all.

The first time I played golf on an actual golf course was with Uncle Paul. He was good, I was not. Eventually, through the years, he would end up shooting his age over a hundred times, which is a goal most humans hope to do once in their lives. Anyway, this first time I played with him, I learned my first lesson on the very first hole out at the course in Lumber Bridge, NC near where I grew up. He hit his first ball down the middle and then I stepped up to the first tee and zonked one into the rough. We walked over to my ball and Uncle Paul gave me the appropriate club to use and then I reached down to move the ball out of the thick grass so I could hit it better. "What are you doing?" He asked me.

"I'm just moving it a little so I can hit it."

"No, Gary, we don't do that in golf. We play it as it lies."

I nodded and then looked down at my ball which was surrounded by high grass, and said, "But it would help me if I could just move it a little bit, not closer to the hole, just out of this high grass."

"Gary," he said, not smiling at all, "wrong is wrong even when it helps you."

So, I chunked it out of the high grass and we finished our round that day. Uncle Paul never said any bad words at all, which is very hard to do when you play golf. I didn't say any either because I didn't want Uncle Paul to hear me. Also, I only knew about three bad words at that time in my life and I didn't really know what they meant. It was a great day. When we got back to the car and loaded the clubs in the trunk, Uncle Paul asked me if I had fun.

"Yes! I loved it! But . . . golf sure is hard, isn't it?"

He smiled and looked over at me and answered, "Everything is hard before it's easy."

I wasn't entirely certain what that meant but if Uncle Paul said it, then I believed it. He continued to play golf with me every month or so and also continued to teach me things that I would remember throughout my life, although I didn't realize at the time he WAS teaching me anything. It was only later, and even today, that I still utilize some of the things I imagine I acquired from him by osmosis.

I'm old now. Sounds bad but it's not really. I've played golf on and off throughout the years. At one point in my life, I was pretty good. Now, who knows from one day to the next what's going to happen. The only thing I'm certain of is that age always wins. I've joined a local golf club and have the opportunity to play several times each week. I've met some interesting guys at the course and have learned a lot of new cuss words. In actuality, I don't think I get nearly enough credit on the course for all the things I manage not to say. Golf can do that to you. In golf and life, there are easy and fun times, then there are difficult and awful times. I've often seen parallels in them both in my life and on the course.

Each of the eighteen holes at Maple Chase, my home course, is different. Some vastly different, as in life. All your years and experiences are different. It's up to you to play the right shot, do the best you can, make good decisions, accept the results, good and bad, and keep on playing. Try not to cuss too much, try not to cheat, try to be fair and good, and be the best you can be. It ain't easy. I'm going to go through each of the holes at Maple Chase and describe them as they are, describe them as I sometimes see them, and describe how life corresponds accordingly to what we think we see and to how it really is. I'll give some insight from some of my new friends at the course, like Roger, Arthur, Bill, Gary, Ben, Gordon, Warren, etc., too many to name, and also from the one man who started it all: Uncle Paul.

First of all, let me list several definitions of golf that I've heard from various players at Maple Chase:

Roger defines it as an endless series of tragedies obscured by the occasional miracle, followed by a good bottle of beer.

Arthur's definition of golf is: You hit down to make the ball go up. You swing left and the ball goes right. The lowest score wins. On top of that, the winner buys the drinks. Crazy!

Bill's summary is this: In golf, a "gimme" can best be defined as an agreement between two golfers . . . neither of whom can putt very well.

And, my favorite description of golf comes from my friend Gary, who says that the most interesting thing about golf is that no matter how badly you play, it is always possible to get worse.

* * *

Then, there are David Letterman's Top Reasons Why Golf Is Better Than Sex . . .

"A below-par performance is considered darn good.

You can stop in the middle and have a cheeseburger and a couple of beers.

It's much easier to find the sweet spot.

Foursomes are encouraged.

You can still make money doing it as a senior.

Three times a day is possible.

Your partner doesn't hire a lawyer if you play with someone else.

You don't have to cuddle with your partner when you're finished.

And, when your equipment gets old, you can replace it."

Several years ago, well, a lot of years ago, I played for the club championship at Pinebrook, which is now Maple Chase. I had an incident happen during that final round that is very similar to the one in the following story. Not exactly, but pretty close. Here's the story:

These two guys were playing for the club championship (not at Maple Chase) and they came to the 18th hole tied for the lead. Lance hit his drive straight down the middle and very long. He only had a short iron left to the green. His opponent, Jerry, sent his tee shot way off-line into the deep woods and brush. They both went over and searched through the rough and trees for Jerry's ball for over ten minutes but they just couldn't find it. Jerry told Lance to go back out to the fairway and play his shot. Lance hits a beautiful shot onto the green about ten feet from the hole. Then, as he's putting his club back into the bag, he hears Jerry yell out, "Found it!" Soon, Jerry's ball comes flying out of the woods and lands on the green about three feet from the hole. Now . . . here's Lance's dilemma: Does he take that cheating, son of a gun's ball out of his pocket? Or, does he just keep his mouth shut?

But, it's not only golfers who are faced with these situations; it's all of us, every day. God gave us the Ten Commandments to live by, but heck, let's not fool ourselves . . . we can't keep Ten

Commandments! Heck, we can't even keep seven or eight; not even four or five of them. I dare to say that most, if not all of us, can't even keep two of the Ten Commandments: Don't lie and don't covet. We can't do it! Don't lie and tell me you can.

I had a boss, years ago, who I played with in a company golf event. He was terrible but he was the boss, so you didn't say anything. On the first hole, he topped his tee shot and it went about forty yards. Then, he hit his second shot in the woods and couldn't find it. He laid out a second ball and shanked it up into a sand trap. It took him two shots to get out of the sand and then he four-putted from about eighteen feet. My friend, Bill, who was keeping the scorecard, asked, "Boss, what did you have on that hole?"

Our boss, leader of the company, and the man you trusted with your career, said, "Ahh, just give me a five." That's golf and that's life. We're all that way, in various forms. If anyone ever tells you to "be yourself," don't! They're giving you bad advice.

#1

Maple Chase Golf & Country Club is a par 72 course. In my opinion, the front nine and the back nine are very different, as in life. The front part of your life is fun and happy and not very hard. But, like at Maple Chase, the back nine of your life can have its challenges: hills and valleys, seemingly impossible obstacles, all fraught with pain and suffering (I might be exaggerating a little).

Hole #1 at The Chase (as our course is affectionately called) is, at first glance, a pretty straightforward par 4 hole that doesn't present many challenges. A good starting point to begin your journey. However, as in life, if you don't make good decisions, you can and will find yourself in a world of trouble. First of all, there's a big tree right in the middle of the fairway. Now, if you're young and strong and good, you can drive your golf ball past that tree and it won't bother you. But . . . if you're not young and strong and good, that tree will be right in your way and prevent you from hitting your second shot to the green.

Also, the green has sand traps on the right-hand side, where most of us slice the ball, which seem to beckon all wayward shots. Then, if you somehow can avoid the tree and the sand traps, but hit it a little long, the ground just over the green slopes downhill very quickly and steeply. Hit it over the green and you will pay a steep price for that mistake.

So, what seems like a pretty innocuous hole to start your journey on, one with few hazards and challenges, can very quickly get you in a world of trouble if you're not careful. Just like in life. When we're young and stupid, as we all are, the world seems like one big adventure to us. Open and easy with very few obstacles. Nearly everyone I knew back at the beginning saw life as easy and fun and posing very little threat. Just like hole #1.

You get through high school and the world seems like it's yours for the taking. Some go off to college to become the next CEO, or high-priced lawyer, or world-famous doctor, and some finish high school and marry their sweethearts and start families and begin to live the dream. Yep, just like standing on that first tee and looking down that fairway . . . everything looks so free and easy. Until you hit your first shot!

When you're young, you look at things differently than when you're old. A young guy and an older guy can see the same thing yet view it completely differently. I was reminded of the story of a man in his senior years who was walking beside a lake when he suddenly heard a voice:

"Hey, you!" Someone said, "Come over here and kiss me and I'll turn into a beautiful princess."

He looked around but didn't see anyone. Again, a voice said, "Hey, you! Kiss me and I'll turn into a beautiful princess."

Then he noticed a little frog by the water's edge. The frog said, "Hey, you! Kiss me and I'll turn into a beautiful princess."

So, the man reached down, carefully picked up the frog, and put it into his shirt pocket. Then he turned and walked away.

The frog called out, "Hey, didn't you hear what I said? I said, 'Kiss me and I'll turn into a beautiful princess.'"

The man replied, "At my age, I'd rather have a talking frog."

***

Hole #1 . . . here are the questions we must ask ourselves: Are we strong enough to hit it past the tree in the middle of the fairway so we'll have a clear shot to the green? Can we keep it in the middle and not go too far left or go too far right? If so, can we hit our second shot straight and not slice it into the sand trap, or go too far and miss the green entirely? Not only are these golfing questions, but they are also life and living questions. How we answer these and start our life journey is very important. Everything in life prepares you for something else.

I was playing one day with my friend Warren and I hit a beautiful shot on the first hole, down the middle and well past the tree. Warren said, "Nice ball." I smiled and agreed with him.

Then he hit his first shot and pulled it almost off the fairway into the driving range. He angrily blurted out, "Look what you made me do!"

"What?" I answered, "It's not my fault you hit that awful shot."

Warren smiled and replied, "I didn't say it was your fault, I said I was blaming you."

Has that ever happened to you? Someone makes a mistake and tries to blame you for their failure? If not, just wait, it'll happen, probably sooner than later. Husbands blame wives, children blame their parents, guys blame their bosses, everybody blames somebody . . . anybody, rather than placing the blame for their failures where it belongs—on their own shoulders. It's human nature. We all think we're good, some of us even think we're the best! Nothing can ever be our fault . . . no way.

Speaking of my friend Warren, he told me a great joke walking down the fairway one day, just to prove that golf and life don't always have to be so serious. Interestingly enough, they can both be fun . . . if you try hard enough.

As told by Warren, "An old farmer went to town to see a movie. The ticket agent asked him, 'Sir, what's that on your shoulder?'

The old farmer said, 'Oh, that's my pet rooster, Chucky. Wherever I go, Chucky goes.'

'I am sorry, sir,' said the ticket agent. 'We can't allow animals in the theater.'

The old farmer went around the corner and stuffed the bird down his overalls. He returned to the booth, bought a ticket, and entered the theater. He sat down next to two old widows named Mildred and Marge.

The movie started and the rooster began to squirm. The old farmer unbuttoned his fly so Chucky could stick his head out and watch the movie.

'Marge,' whispered Mildred.

'What?' said Marge.

'I think the guy next to me is a pervert.'

Marge asked, 'What makes you think so?'

'He undid his pants and he has his thing out,' whispered Mildred.

'Well, don't worry about it,' said Marge. 'Heck, at our age we've seen 'em all.'

'I thought so too,' said Mildred, 'but this one's eatin' my popcorn!'"

***

Back to golf… and life. I used to think that when I made a bogey on hole #1 that my round was ruined. One hole and already one over par. It made me mad. But, if I made a par on the first hole, or even better yet, a birdie, then I was excited. However, none of those sensations lasted long. As in life, you simply can't let a failure, or setback, or even a victory determine how you go about living your life. Each hole is different, each day is different, all decisions and all shots are important. Sometimes, especially when we're young, we think we're making good decisions, but in retrospect, they may not have been the best choices. And sometimes your decisions are taken from you by someone else, as in the case of my friend A.C.

He married the girl of his dreams when he was a young man and thought his life was set. They immediately had three boys, which started putting a drain on the finances of their family. A.C. told his wife he didn't think they should have any more children since they could barely afford the ones they already had, but his wife wanted more and they argued about it. Finally, A.C. didn't think he'd ever win that argument, so he went and had a vasectomy without his wife's knowledge. Low and behold, several months later she became pregnant! She swore the baby was A.C.'s and it led to unpleasant results.

This pregnancy led to her leaving her boys and A.C. and going to court to demand child support for her new baby. At the trial, A.C. produced the documents of his vasectomy and the judge ruled in his favor. His ex-wife then married her lover and father of her newest baby.

But, A.C. didn't let this unpleasant start ruin his life. He continued to work hard, raise his sons, become a successful businessman, and marry another lady who has now been with him more than thirty years. And, he's a pretty good golfer.

Conversely, my friend Michael had it all given to him. His parents spoiled him rotten. He was given everything from an early age. He had a new Corvette when the rest of us were still riding broken-down bicycles. He always had new loafers, pressed shirts and pants, and the best that money could buy. Certainly, Michael had it all. Then he starting dating one of the prettiest girls in our class and that really made us all jealous. What a start to a charming and successful life. Or so we thought.

Michael's start never gained any traction. He kept waiting for someone to give him more and more: for his parents to keep giving to him; for his wife to work for him. When those two options didn't pan out, he started gambling to make others pay him, but all he did was lose. He eventually lost it all. His wife left him, his health left him, and what little money he had was owed to the bookies. The great start he was blessed with ended up in a shortened, tragic life, ended by health failures, financial failures, and personal failures.

The first hole is important . . . but, it's only the first hole. You can follow Michael's example or follow A.C.'s example. Or any of a thousand others; the decision is yours. On the golf course, you have seventeen more holes to play; and in life, you have the rest of it to live and plan for. It's all up to you.

#2

The second hole at Maple Chase is a par 3 on the scorecard. The problem is that actually making a par 3 on this hole is very tough. For me, it's usually a par 4, with several unutterable cuss words thrown in. From the white tees, it's usually about 173 yards to a green guarded on the front left by a menacing bunker, and just over the green is another less menacing bunker. And, I should mention that there is a creek between the tee and the green. The creek really should not come in play . . . it really shouldn't. Just like it shouldn't matter if you finish school, or go to college, or just get a job at Food Lion.

Heck, we've still got our whole lives in front of us; we can do whatever we want. So what if we happen to dump one in the creek, we've still got sixteen holes left to get things in order. Plenty of time. You would think that this creek, which is just over halfway to the green, would never come into play. You would be wrong. I've seen very good players dump their tee shots into this creek. I've dumped tee balls into this creek. I've seen A.C., Roger, Gordon, Arthur, Bill, Gary, and Ben all dump balls into the creek. We hit them fat, we top them, we slice them, we do everything but the right thing, and into the creek they go.

We should've been more careful. We should have stayed in school longer. We should have worked harder, saved more, invested better; we should've left that one girl alone—no matter how short her skirt was. Ah, but we're young, we're just starting out. We have plenty of time to make up for our mistakes . . . right? We're young, we've got plenty of time to make amends, and we're tough! I thought I was tough as well until my friend Dickie told me a story about a real badass:

Ever heard of Ernest Hemingway? If you're young, you probably haven't. He isn't on Twitter or Facebook or Instagram. But most of us older people have heard of him. Yeah, I remember him . . . he wrote a few books, didn't he? Yes, he did. He also lived through a mortar attack, anthrax, malaria, pneumonia, dysentery, skin cancer, hepatitis, diabetes, two plane crashes, three car accidents, first and second-degree burns, a ruptured kidney, liver, and spleen, a crushed vertebra, and a fractured skull. But he never stopped. He kept writing.

Last week, I hit my tee shot on this second hole into the left side bunker; then, I blasted out over the green into the back bunker. I got out of that one okay, then two-putted for a sweet double-bogey five on this little hole. After I slammed my club into the ground, cussed out Jerry (he deserved it), and spit on my shoes by accident, I was ready to quit and go home. Golf sucks! But I couldn't quit; I still had sixteen holes left to play. I asked for forgiveness for my bad temper; I needed to forget this hole. After all, a clear conscience is usually the sign of a bad memory.

I just needed to toughen up and be strong, like Ernest Hemingway . . . or Audie Murphy. Remember him? He is most remembered as a Hollywood star for over twenty-one years. But what I remember him for is something entirely different. He was one of the most decorated American combat soldiers of World War II. He received every combat award for valor available from the U.S Army, as well as French and Belgian awards for heroism.

After the attack on Pearl Harbor in 1941, his sister helped him to falsify documentation about his birthdate in order to meet the minimum age requirement for enlisting in the military. He was initially turned down by the Army, Navy, and the Marine Corps for being underweight. He was eventually allowed to enlist in the Army and saw his first action in the 1943 Allied invasion of Sicily. He subsequently saw repeated action throughout Europe.

In 1944, he encountered a German machine gun crew who pretended they were surrendering, then shot his best buddy who was standing next to him. Murphy killed everyone in the gun nest, then used their weaponry to kill every German in a 100-yard radius, including two more machine gun nests and a bunch of snipers. In another battle, he jumped into a burning M-10 tank destroyer and used it to annihilate every enemy in sight, then leaped clear before it exploded, all while he had malaria. What a man! Oh, I almost forgot to mention that Audie Murphy did all this when he was 16 years old, 5'5" in height, and weighing only 110 pounds.

You don't have to hit the ball 300 yards, or be able to slice or draw your iron shots, or even be able to putt like Jordan Spieth. You just need a heart and a desire to do the right thing and never give up. Don't quit after a double-bogey on the second hole. Keep going. Don't give up, right Jimmy V? Don't ever give up.

***

My friend Arthur is a good example of someone who never gave up, then or now. Arthur is 83 years old and still WALKS 18 holes with us each week, pushing his cart up and down those rugged hills on the back nine. Sometimes I even catch him singing an old Otis Redding or Temptations song as he's walking up the fairway.

Given his circumstances, it would have been fairly easy for Arthur to give up on himself. He was born the last of eleven children to a sharecropper family in rural Alabama. There were so many kids in his small house that Arthur walked down the road a couple of miles to his grandparent's house one day just to have some quiet. He stayed there several years, according to him, and no one even noticed he was missing . . . I doubt that. He could have resigned himself to that life and given up. After all, isn't that what a poor sharecropper's son was expected to do in rural Alabama seventy or eighty years ago?

Not Arthur!

He decided he wouldn't give up, that he wouldn't quit, even after being in the sand trap and double-bogeying the first hole. No! He'd keep on going and par this course called life. Heck, he'd even go under par . . . why not?

He did well in school and attended a HBCU college and graduated. However, more important than graduating, he met his future wife there, who just happened to be the youngest of seventeen children. Yes, 17. They each graduated, got married, and started the journey of never giving up. She became a teacher and Arthur joined the Air Force. While serving his country, here and in Vietnam, he also kept pursuing his education and received his master's degree while still in the Air Force. Then, just to ensure a birdie on the next hole, he kept going and completed his Ph.D. in Economics.

Upon retiring from the Air Force, Arthur started teaching Economics at Baylor University while his wife kept busy teaching and raising two sons. Then, Winston-Salem State University came calling and lured Arthur here to Winston-

Salem to head the Economics Department. Now, fully retired and being only the fourth person ever to be awarded Winston-Salem State's Emeritus status, he plays golf with us and hums golden oldies to us as we amble down the fairway.

A couple of years ago, Arthur's wife died. It was pretty sudden and left Arthur with a big hole in his life. Months went by as he tried to tie up all loose ends and figure out how to keep going by himself. His friend and neighbor, and my golfing buddy, Roger, saw him one day out in the yard and began nagging him to come back out to the golf course and playing with him one day. Roger told me he had not been playing well and his scores were getting closer and closer to 90.

He finally convinced Arthur to join him one day and they both walked the fairways and talked about life and family and what it all means. That day, Roger shot 78, breaking 80 for the first time in a long time. I wish I could've been there and listened to the conversations between them that day. I'm sure old Arthur topped a few shots and said, "Look up and you'll see a bad shot every time." But ... he never gave up. Roger never gave up. And that story should give us all inspiration to "never give up."

#3

It's hard to talk about golf, and life, without remembering a few good jokes. If you take either one of them too seriously, you'll be a grouch and very unhappy, like my friend . . . who shall remain nameless. So, before we get to hole #3, let's start with a joke—you can determine if it's good or not:

  An old golfer comes from a round of golf at a new course and heads into the grill room.As he passes through the swinging doors, he sees a sign hanging over the bar:

COLD BEER: $2.00
HAMBURGER: $2.25
CHEESEBURGER: $2.50
CHICKEN SANDWICH: $3.50
HAND JOB: $50.00

Checking his wallet to be sure he has the necessary payment, the old golfer walks up to the bar and beckons to the exceptionally attractive female bartender who is serving drinks to a couple of sun-wrinkled golfers. She glides down behind the bar to the old golfer.

"Yes?" She inquires with a wide, knowing smile, "May I help you?"

The old golfer leans over the bar and whispers,

"I was wondering, young lady," he whispers, "are you the one who gives the hand-jobs?"

She looks into his eyes with that wide smile and purrs: "Yes Sir, I sure am."

The old golfer leans closer and into her left ear he says softly, "Well, wash your hands real good because I want a cheeseburger."

Hole #3 at Maple Chase is a simple hole . . . that's what makes it so hard. Just like life, when you think your life is simple and easy, things can turn into crap in no time flat. One bad decision, one mistake, one wrong turn, and your simple, easy life can turn into a nightmare.

The third hole is a par 4 with deep woods down the right-hand side of the fairway and a menacing, treacherous creek down the left-hand side and in front of the green. What makes it so difficult is that the creek is only about five feet in front of the green. If you hit your shot five feet short, you are in the creek! But, if you are too careful and hit it long, then there are mounds and hills over the green, which make it nearly impossible to chip back close to the pin.

As in life, if you come up a bit short on your goals and expectations, you can find yourself in the creek, in more ways than one. The high school senior who planned to go to college, but came up a bit short on the SATs and never followed through. The prom queens who only wanted to have a "bit of fun" on prom night and found themselves pregnant at eighteen years old. The young couple who thought they found true love and rushed off to get married at nineteen years old, only to find that the man, or woman, they thought they were marrying was not exactly the person of their dreams.

And, conversely, the man who waited too long and missed out on every opportunity to be happy. My friend Mike is the perfect example. Right after high school he lucked into a really nice job and put off going to college for "a year or two." He kept working, making pretty good money, and never followed his college dream. He met a girl at some club, fell in lust, and got married. Then, fell out of lust and got divorced. However, she had a better lawyer than he did, so he lost more than her intimacy in the ensuing legal proceedings.

That reminds me of a lawyer story I once heard:

The madam opened the brothel door in Butte, Montana, and saw a rather dignified, well-dressed, good-looking man in his late fifties. "May I help you, sir?" she asked.

The man replied, "I want to see Valerie."

"Sir, Valerie is one of our most expensive ladies. Perhaps you would prefer someone else," said the madam.

"No, I must see Valerie."

Just then, the gorgeous Valerie appeared and announced to the man that she charged $5,000 a visit. Without hesitation, the man pulled out five thousand dollars and gave it to Valerie, and they went upstairs. After an hour, the man calmly left.

The next night, the man appeared again, once more demanding to see Valerie. Valerie explained that no one had ever come back two nights in a row as she was too expensive. "There are no discounts. The price is still $5,000."

Again, the man pulled out the money, gave it to Valerie, and they went upstairs. After an hour, he left.

The following night the man was there yet again. Everyone was astounded that he had come for a third consecutive night, but he paid Valerie and they went upstairs. After their session, Valerie said to the man, "No one has ever been with me three nights in a row. Where are you from?"
The man replied, "Great Falls."
"Really," she said. "I have family in Great Falls."
"I know," the man answered. "Your sister died and I am her attorney. She asked me to give you your $15,000 inheritance."
The moral of this story is that three things in life are certain:
1. Death,
2. Taxes, and
3. Being screwed by a lawyer

***

In life, we sometimes don't know what's around the corner waiting for us. We never know there is a creek just ahead of us, waiting to gobble up wayward shots or bad decisions. Sometimes, through no fault of our own, we make mistakes just because we don't know. An example of not knowing is this: George Washington died in 1799. The first dinosaur fossil wasn't discovered until 1824. George Washington never knew dinosaurs existed!

At other times in our lives, some things and circumstances occur that seem too crazy to be true. As an example: The United States is roughly 3,000 miles wide. The Amazon River, in South America, is over 4,300 miles long, yet there is not one bridge across that river. Not one! Would you have ever believed it? Would you have ever believed you would have had five children before you were thirty? Or, that you would keep the same job your entire life? Or, that you would have believed this or that? No, that's what life does to us; it keeps giving us the unexpected, it keeps the creek always in front of us. It's never easy.

I'm sure a Russian peasant girl, named Valentina Vassilyev, who lived in the eighteenth century, would have never believed she would have had 69 babies from 1725 to 1765! 67 of the babies survived infancy. She had 16 pairs of twins. We never know what life will bring us. That's why we must prepare, we must learn, we must be ready to cope with all sorts of things.

Always use a golf club that will get you over the creek. But, always know that hills and mounds are waiting for you. It will seldom be easy. Life will throw darts at you. Challenges will come out of nowhere. You must plan and always be prepared for the unknown, the unplanned, the unexpected. You can do everything right and still bad stuff will happen to you.

One of baseball's best pitchers ever is a great example of this. In pitching, your earned run average, or ERA, is commonly known as the best way to judge how good a pitcher is. His won/lost record is also a good way to judge his performance. Any pitcher who has an ERA under 4.0 is generally thought to be a good pitcher. If he has an ERA under 3.0, he is considered to be a GREAT pitcher.

Tom Seaver had a total of 94 losses in the Major Leagues. In those 94 losses, his record, of course, was 0-94, but with a 2.74 ERA. Yeah, his team lost those 94 games but he pitched extremely well. The same thing will happen to you. You will do great and yet bad things will happen. Someone else will get the promotion you should have gotten. Your best friend will marry the pretty girl that you thought you should have married. Your kid will get passed over for a scholarship, or not start on the tennis team, or any other myriad of things that will come your way. Life ain't fair. It never was and it never will be. Just do the best you can, plan for things, don't get too discouraged. Just get over the creek and see what happens . . . heck, you might even make a birdie!

#4

The fourth hole at Maple Chase is a par 4, dogleg to the right, with a creek on the right side of the fairway. It's the same creek that runs in front of #3. This menacing little creek is not content to gobble up all errant shots on the previous hole, it now has to attract all shots not hit perfectly straight on the next hole. Totally unfair! But, when is golf, or life, fair? I'm still waiting. I know of so many stories of the "unfairness" of life. One that breaks my heart is the true story of a pine tree that was planted in 2004 in memory of former Beatle George Harrison. The tree died after being infested with beetles. Now that just ain't right!

But back to golf . . . hole #4 is tough because you just can't risk hitting near the creek; you have to hit away from the creek, which means you are hitting away from your target-- the green. Oh, you can try to cut the corner, but trust me, you'll pay the price. Just as in life. Try to take the easy way or the simple way, and you'll pay the price. Maybe not today or tomorrow, but you'll pay eventually.

Don't go to college, take the easy way out, and just find yourself a nice job and start working; yeah, everything will be fine. Don't put in the extra time at work, just leave as soon as you can—no one will notice. Find a nice, pretty girl but don't treat her any differently than all the other girls—she'll wait for you. You have plenty of time. And absolutely don't waste any of your money on saving accounts or investments! Plenty of time for that. Have fun! Make hay while you can. Enjoy life, see the world. You can always save . . . later.

If you try to cut the corner on that dogleg at hole #4, you might make it once or twice, or even three or four times. But trust me; it WILL get you. That creek is waiting for all of us who just can't play it safe, for those of us willing to risk it all, instead of doing the smart thing. My friend Roger has fished out hundreds of balls from that creek. He loves that creek. All his grandchildren have more golf balls than they'll ever need in their lives . . . because people are greedy and don't think. They want to take the shortcut, they're not willing to play it safe, to do the smart thing. They're sure, they're certain, they are so confident that little creek will not harm them. Keep on believing . . . Roger loves it!

I hit balls in that creek four rounds in a row. Four! I wasn't trying to cut the corner or take any shortcuts; I just sliced the ball and there it went like it was a magnet sucking my ball into the depths of despair. One day, as I was getting ready to tee my ball up, I looked over at Roger (who never hits a ball into the creek), held my ball up toward him, and said, "Roger, please tell my ball to stay AWAY from that creek."

Roger said, "Ball, I'm telling you now, 'Stay out of that creek.'" And you know what? It did. I hit a beautiful shot down the middle, well away from the creek. I smiled at Roger and he nodded at me. The next round I did the same thing: I asked Roger to warn my ball, he did, and I hit another beautiful shot down the middle. Then, the next round, being so sure of myself and over-confident in my abilities, I didn't ask Roger. Do I need to finish this story? Of course not! You know what happened.

Fortunately for me, Roger got his ball retriever and fished out my ball from the creek. Before I even dried it off, I looked at it and asked, "Why? Why did you do that?"

It didn't answer me, but my friend, Ben, did. He said, "Why did the chicken cross the road?" As I was waiting for his answer, he walked away. Later that night I started wondering why DID that chicken cross the road? I researched it, I Googled it, I even asked Jerry, and these are the answers I found from some very smart and famous people:

DONALD TRUMP: I've been told by many sources, good sources—they're very good sources—that the chicken crossed the road. All the Fake News wants to do is write nasty things about the road, but it's really a good road. It's a beautiful road. Everyone knows how beautiful it is.

JOE BIDEN: Why did the chicken do the . . . thing in the . . . you know the rest.

BARACK OBAMA: Let me be perfectly clear, if the chickens like their eggs they can keep their eggs. No chicken will be required to cross the road to surrender her eggs. Period.

AOC: Chickens should not be forced to lay eggs! This is because of corporate greed! Eggs should be able to lay themselves.

HILLARY CLINTON: What difference at this point does it make why the chicken crossed the road?

DICK CHENEY: Where's my gun?

BILL CLINTON: I did not cross the road with that chicken.

JOHN KERRY: Although I voted to let the chicken cross the road, I am now against it! It was the wrong road to cross, and I was misled about the chicken's intentions. I am not for it now and will remain against it.

AL SHARPTON: Why are all the chickens white?

ANDERSON COOPER: We have reason to believe there is a chicken, but we have not yet been allowed to have access to the other side of the road.

NANCY GRACE: That chicken crossed the road because he's guilty! You can see it in his eyes and the way he walks.

PAT BUCHANAN: To steal the job of a decent, hardworking American.

MARTHA STEWART: No one called me to warn me which way the chicken was going. I had a standing order at the Farmer's Market to sell my eggs when the price dropped to a certain level. No little bird gave me any insider information.

ERNEST HEMINGWAY: To die in the rain, alone.

COLONEL SANDERS: Did I miss one?

***

If you're lucky enough to find the fairway on hole #4, you then have a rather simple shot to the green. The problem is determining which golf club to use for this shot. The green is long and the pin can be in the front or back or the middle of the green. If you're standing at the 150-yard marker and hit a 150-yard shot, but the pin is at the back of the green, you're in trouble. You are still about thirty or forty feet from the pin with a large hill to navigate. It's very hard for most of us to putt the ball accurately with those conditions.

However, if you plan, or, if you're smart, you won't pay attention to what the yardage marker in the fairway says. You will have a hand-held device that measures the distance to the pin for you—or else, ask Roger, as I do. If you're at the 150-yard marker in the fairway, your second shot could be 130 yards, 140 yards, 150 yards, or 160 yards . . . depending on where the pin is located. To be successful, you must do your homework and know exactly what the distance is. Or else, you could hit a very nice shot and still be forty feet away.

Just like in your life, you can't take for granted what you "think" you see. You must study the facts, ask questions, gain experience, or use the experience of others before you make decisions. Those of us who don't usually end up having forty-five-foot putts, where the smart player only has ten feet left. A lot of times, especially when we're younger, we tend to think we know it all, that we have all the answers and we don't need anyone interfering with our lives.

After all, what does your old dad know? Things are different today than they were twenty or thirty years ago, right? Yeah, I'll be fine. I'll work a year or two, then I'll buy a nice car, save some money, then I'll go to college when I can afford it. Everything will be great. Oh, man . . . how many times do I wish I'd asked ole' Roger exactly how far that pin actually was? But, I didn't; I find myself in the same predicament as most Americans—just not knowing.

Americans may lead the world in thinking they know everything, when in fact, we don't. A good example of this is that 46% of Americans don't know how long it takes the earth to go around the sun. And even worse, about 1 in 4 Americans aren't sure if the earth travels around the sun or vice versa. I asked my friend David one time what was the largest state EAST of the Mississippi River. His answer: Montana.

"Montana?" I asked.

"Yep, got to be, that's a large state."

"East of the Mississippi River?" I asked again.

"Mmm . . . yep."

Now, old David has a college degree, was a very successful businessman, and is, apparently, a very smart man. Well, everything is hard before it's easy. I stared at old David and asked, "Are you sure there's not another answer inside of you?"

He took a sip of something from inside his golf cart and said, "Only God knows what's really inside me . . . and I hope He never tells anyone."

***

We, as Americans, should be very proud of our country. I love America. Do we have faults? Of course we do. But we're free and people can basically do almost whatever they want to do. It's not like that in most places in the world. I was traveling a couple of years ago and we were in Tallinn, Estonia (yeah, I'd never heard of it either). It's sort of between Lithuania and Russia, on the Baltic Sea. A beautiful little town.

We were in one of the little shops there and the young girl behind the counter looked to be about 19 years old. I found a little wooden box I wanted to buy but it didn't have a price on it. I wondered how I would communicate with this young girl . . . heck, I didn't know if she spoke Estonian or what? I walked up to her and held the box out and said very slowly, "How much is this?"

She took the box and answered in better English than most of my family speaks. I was very surprised and asked her how she learned English so well. She said, "I learned from watching TV."

I asked what her native language was and she told me, "We speak Estonian, German, Russian, and English."

Heck, I was proud of myself because I can say "Hola, adios, and taco" in Spanish.

One other story and I'll let this go. Several years ago, my wife and I were in a small, remote little village in western Ireland. I don't even remember the name of it. It wasn't a place that attracts tourists; it's just an out-of-the-way place you might pass through on the way to somewhere else. It was getting late in the day and we were tired and thirsty and longing for a Guinness, so we stopped at the little pub off the side of the street.

We weren't sure it was even open until we walked in and saw an older woman behind the bar and an old man asleep at a table. She brought us a Guinness and started talking to us and asking us questions when a younger woman with a little girl walked in the front door. It was the older woman's daughter and granddaughter. The granddaughter was about ten years old and very pretty.
The grandmother introduced them to us and my wife said, in her southern accent, "So nice to meet you. Your grandmother told us all about you."

The little girl looked very surprised and excitedly asked, "Are you from North Carolina? I love North Carolina?"

We hadn't told her anything about us. She had just walked in the door. We were shocked. Apparently, she knew about Southern accents and Southern states and she was excited to meet a man and woman from America. Why she mentioned North Carolina instead of South Carolina, or Georgia, or God-forbid, Alabama . . . I have no idea. But she did. And what this little story has to do with hole #4 at Maple Chase, I also have no idea. But here it is.

#5

Hole #5 is a par three, however, actually making a par three on this hole is very difficult. From the white tees, where I play from, it's about 170 yards or so, depending on where the tee markers are set up and where the pin is located. The green is greatly sloped from right to left and not very deep. Therefore, there are only two flat places the pin can be placed: up high on the right-hand side, or down low on the left-hand side. The complete middle section of the green is one big slope: You are either putting up the hill or down the hill.

Similar to life, in which it seems nearly all of us are always putting up the hill. Not all of us, however, some people have life handed to them on a silver platter. I don't know any of them. I heard the story of such a man at our course, and I truly don't know his name, but my friend A.C. told me about him. He said this "blue-blood" was a real jerk and that he constantly ridiculed him and teased him. Someone told A.C. that this guy was an only child and that his family was rich and he had never had to work. One day, old A.C. had enough of this taunting and told the guy if he opened his mouth again that he was going to punch him right in the mouth. The guy stopped.

This was an isolated case. Most guys and girls on the course are very nice and well-mannered. Sure, there's the occasional cuss word after a bad shot-- golf can easily elicit those responses. The most common phrase I've heard, from just about everyone (even the girls) is "F#%k." Yes, the old "F" word is alive and well. You'd think that a new term would have evolved with new generations, but alas, the "F" word always seems appropriate in certain situations.

In fact, the "F" word is actually one of the oldest sexual euphemisms in the English language, first recorded in 1508. It was briefly replaced in the late 1800s by the term "horizontal entertainment" but that was a few too many syllables to say when you became suddenly mad.

***

This little 5th hole can be extremely frustrating due to its nature. When the pin is set up the hill on the right-hand side, it's very difficult to hit a shot close to the hole. You can hit what looks to be a very good shot, but the ball will not stay up top and will succumb to the effects of gravity and roll all the way down the hill, forty or fifty feet away from the pin. Unless the pin is down low on the left-hand side . . . then, the ball will never roll down the hill. It always stays up top, defying gravity and ignoring every cuss word known to man, often requiring many references to "horizontal entertainment."

Life can also be that way. You're just starting out in business and things are looking good, then, dang, things slowly start going downhill through no fault of your own. You've planned well, you did your research, you worked hard, and it was all looking good. But just like your tee shot to that pin, up top, on the right-hand side . . . when that ball starts it's slow, painful trip down the hill . . . there's nothing you can do about it. You did nothing wrong. You hit a good shot. You executed your plan almost to perfection, but still, you'll pay a painful price. It ain't fair! All you can do is to exclaim, "horizontal entertainment."

But you can't let this misfortune linger and affect your life or your game. Just accept your fate, try to get over it, and move on, doing your best. My friend Ben is one of the best at this I've ever seen. He doesn't hit many bad shots, but when he does, he quickly forgets it and keeps going. I never see Ben slam his club into the ground, like I do; or throw his club, like I do; or use the "F" word, like I do. What is wrong with Ben?

One day, when the pin was at the bottom left, I hit a shot up near the top of the green to the right. And guess what? Correct! The ball stayed up top and never rolled down the hill. Have I mentioned yet that golf is not fair? Just like life. As I walked down the fairway, I started mumbling about how unfair that was, when old Ben came up to me and said that he'd just visited a small zoo in North Carolina. He wanted to get my mind off that shot.

I knew Ben had just moved here from Maryland, so I asked him where this zoo was. He didn't remember the name of the town, but he did say that the zoo had obtained a very rare species of gorilla. The staff had noticed that within a few weeks the gorilla, a female, became very difficult to handle. Upon examination, the veterinarian determined the problem. The gorilla was in heat. To make matters worse, there was no male gorilla available.

Thinking about their problem, the zookeeper thought of Bobby Lee Walton, a redneck part-time worker responsible for cleaning the animal cages. Bobby Lee, like not a few rednecks, had little sense but possessed ample ability to satisfy a female of any species. The zookeeper thought they might have a solution:

Bobby Lee was approached with a proposition. Would he be willing to mate with the gorilla for $500.00? Bobby Lee showed some interest but said he would have to think the matter over carefully. The following day, he announced that he would accept their offer, but only under five conditions.

"First," Bobby Lee said, "I ain't gonna kiss her on the lips." The keeper quickly agreed to this condition.

"Second," he said, "She must wear a 'Dale Earnhardt Forever' t-shirt." The keeper again readily agreed to this condition.

"Third," he said, "You can't never tell nobody about this." The keeper again readily agreed to this condition.

"Fourth," Bobby Lee said, "I want all the children raised Southern Baptist." Once again, it was agreed.

"And last," Bobby Lee said, "I'm gonna need another week to come up with the $500.00."

By the time we reached the green, my temper had abated and Ben had me smiling. I still didn't make par, but Ben and Bobby Lee made me enjoy the hole more than I would have.

The one good thing about hole #5 is that there's a bathroom near the green. There's also a reminder posted on the outside wall to make calls to the grill if you want a sandwich or something to drink at the turn. That way, it'll be ready for you when you finish hole #9.

I played nine holes with a gentleman one day, who shall remain nameless, who did not need to call the grill to place an order. He had all he needed in his golf cart. I was walking and he was riding in the cart but he drove next to me so we could talk. He was very nice, very intelligent, and very sociable. He told me one story after another, all of which were either funny, interesting, or informative. At one point, when he got out of the cart to hit a shot, I looked in the golf cart and saw several small liquor bottles, the kind you buy in an airport. Most of them were empty. When he got back in the cart, he opened another of these small bottles and poured it into his cup. He saw me looking at him and asked if I wanted a drink. Before I could answer, he said, "Helps me relax, like it did for George Washington."

"George Washington?" I asked.

"Yeah," he said. "When Washington was leaving the Capitol after his second term, the Founding Fathers threw him a farewell party. The bar tab is still intact. According to the bill, these fifty-five attendees drank 54 bottles of Madeira, 60 bottles of claret, 8 bottles of whiskey, 22 bottles of porter, 8 bottles of hard cider, 12 of beer, and 7 bowls of alcoholic punch. If they could do that and still run our country, I figure I can have a sip or two on the course."

Since my friend was even par after the first five treacherous holes, I firmly agreed with him. Before teeing off on the sixth hole, my friend and I looked back at the green we'd just left. It seems so innocent and simple when you look back at it, makes you wonder why it's so hard. I thought to myself, "Am I thinking about this hole, or am I thinking about life?"

Then, my friend added, "Don't look back. You're not going that way."

I smiled at him and said, "Thanks for the words of wisdom."

He took a small drink and replied, "A word to the wise ain't necessary—it's the stupid ones that need the advice."

I wasn't really sure in which of these two categories I fit, so I smiled again and we headed on to the next hole.

#6

The sixth hole at Maple Chase is a par 5 and is also the number one handicap hole on the course—which means it's the hardest hole to par. It's not the longest hole, it's just the hardest hole because the slightest mistake you make can ruin your score. First of all, you must hit your drive over a stream/lake, which also borders the left-hand side of the fairway. But you can't hit away from this lake either because there is high grass and trees on the right-hand side of the fairway. Oh . . . and it's all uphill.

For the big hitters, it's possible to reach the green with your second shot, assuming you're not in the lake or in the woods. For most normal people, it's a lay-up second shot, with the lake on the left-hand side of the fairway and some mounds on the right-hand side. Plus, the fairway doglegs left to the green and there is a steep hill to the left of the green we all call "Death Valley."

The green itself is mainly why this hole is rated the toughest on the course. It's turtle-backed, which means it slopes away from all sides, like the shape of a turtle. There may be about a ten-foot square area to land your ball safely. Otherwise, your ball will roll down into Death Valley, or worse, go over the green, down a steep slope, and end up twenty-five yards away. It's tough. Plus, there's a sand trap to the right of the green that doesn't help.

Bottom line is that you must choose your club carefully. You have to make the right decision on yardage, on picking your landing spot, and on where you don't want to miss, all sort of like the decisions you make when picking a husband or wife. When you're young, there are so many decisions, so many pretty girls to choose from. There are party-girls who love to have fun; glamorous girls who love to dress up, intelligent girls who can intimidate you with their brain power; plain, simple girls who seem like they'd make good mothers and homemakers. And there's always the good girl that all the parents like . . . but, aren't good girls simply bad girls that never got caught? And then there's the girl who sweeps you off your feet.

There's always that one girl out there that's hard to find, like the green on #6. All the other girls are nice, but like your approach shot on this treacherous hole, your advances will roll off the green, down into Death Valley. You keep playing this hole, you keep hitting shots and they roll this way and that way, never seeming to find the target. It's hard.

Sometimes we make bad decisions. We choose the wrong club or choose a girl just because she's pretty . . . or hit the wrong shot or choose a girl because she's good in the backseat of your daddy's car. How do we know we're choosing the right club to hit? This hole is so difficult it can be downright scary. Should I get serious with this girl, or just keep playing the field? Maybe there's someone out there better. Maybe there's someone out there who will appreciate me more and understand how good I am . . . it could happen.

Should I get serious with the girl mom and dad like? Should I chase that pretty girl who flirts with all the boys? Should I settle for the girl who'll make a good mother and housekeeper? I don't want to end up in Death Valley, but I don't want to settle either. Eventually you'll find it all probably comes down to what Woody Allen so famously said: "The heart wants what the heart wants." It won't be your mom's choice, or your friends' choice, or even your own logical choice . . . it'll be your heart's choice.

I know of people who dated for four years, got married, then divorced within a year. I know others who only dated twice— yes, twice—and have stayed married for over thirty years. There is no formula for success. Just like on #6, there is no one club you can use to reach the green. Each person has to evaluate their situation and decide what is right for them. It isn't easy. Sometimes it's downright scary.

Sometimes you hit such a bad drive that you have no choice when hitting to the green. Sometimes you get a girl pregnant and the choice is made for you. Or, your family pressures you into something you're not certain of. Or, your physical desires become overwhelming and you just want someone, ANYONE, to fulfill your fantasies. Heck, I dreamed one time that I hit a ball onto the green at #6 and it actually stayed on the green and didn't roll off! Which reminds me of the time in my dorm room when Lydia came over . . .

***

If you are ever lucky enough to find the right woman, as I have, it'll make the slow walk up the fairway on #6 much less stressful. I can't imagine how guys exist without a woman to shop for them, cook for them, clean for them, make decisions for them, etc., etc., etc. Women are, in fact, amazing; however, they pay a heavy price for taking care of us: 80% of migraine sufferers are women. I wonder why? There was even a young 6-year-old girl in Peru that had a baby one time. And, did you know the 10 longest-living people in history were all women? Why? Because men are stupid.

We all think we can hit a 3-wood 220 yards over a lake and land it on a green the size of a quarter. We're stupid! Case in point: Each year about 1,700 men visit the emergency room with "zipper accidents." We need women! How in the world would we exist without them? When there are no eligible women around, we'll resort to marrying our first cousins— about 20% of all married couples are indeed first cousins.

I was playing hole #6 one day with my lawyer friend, Warren, and he told me a woman story. I can tell this story now because Warren is retired from lawyering and is strictly a golfer these days. We're waiting in the fairway for the group ahead of us to hit their balls out of Death Valley around the green—we knew we'd be there for several minutes. Warren related the following account:

"Two lawyers had been stranded on a desert island for several months. The only thing on the island was a tall coconut tree that provided them their only food. Each day one of the lawyers would climb to the top to see if he could spot a rescue boat coming.

One day the lawyer yelled down from the tree, 'Wow, I just can't believe my eyes. There is a woman out there floating in our direction.'

The lawyer on the ground was most skeptical and said, 'You're hallucinating; you've finally lost your mind.' But within a few minutes, up to the beach floated a stunning redhead, face-up, totally naked, unconscious, without even so much as a ring or earrings on her person.

The two lawyers went down to the water, dragged her up on the beach, and discovered, yes, she was alive, warm, and breathing.

One said to the other, 'You know, we've been on this God-forsaken island for months now without a woman. It's been such a long, long time . . . so . . . do you think we should . . . well . . . you know . . . screw her?'

'Out of WHAT!?' asked the other."

**

Yep, the sixth hole, 1/3 of the way around the course. Where will you be 1/3 of the way through your life? Good job, making a nice salary? Married? Kids? Who knows? Say the average life expectancy is around seventy-five (which I'm going to use because I'm bad at math and this number is easy to divide into thirds) which means at 1/3 of your life, you are around twenty-five years old.

Where were you at twenty-five? I was still in graduate school, single, and as broke as a bum in Las Vegas. My friend Dickie was just graduating college, had already served two years in the Army in Korea, and was working in a department store— and still single, too. My sister had graduated college and was the women's basketball coach at a university. My friend Gary had graduated college, had gotten married, and was starting a family while starting a very good and lucrative job.

Of course, there are others, who I won't name . . . twenty-five years old, no college degrees, in-and-out of low-paying, dead-end jobs, no prospects, no ambitions, and no futures, other than where the beer money will come from for Saturday night. The Lord made us all. Only He knows what's truly inside us. I had a friend years ago—he's dead now. After he'd done another of his crazy stunts, I said, "Michael, what are you doing to yourself?"

For once, he was serious when he looked at me and replied, "I do not know myself, and God forbid that I should."

I thought about that statement: Know thyself. I'm afraid if I really knew myself, I would run away.

One-third of your life has passed . . . where are you? There's still plenty of time to change if you need to. There's plenty of time to pursue your dreams if you want to. And, there's plenty of time to keep on keeping on, if you want to. After all, it's completely up to you what decisions you make—or is it? If God had wanted you otherwise, wouldn't He have created you otherwise?

You may have just birdied #6 and you're feeling great about your score. Or, you may have parred this difficult hole and you're still feeling good. Or, you may have bogeyed it, or double-bogeyed it, or even worse . . . but you know what? You still have at least two-thirds of your life left. Don't stop trying after a couple of bad holes. Hang in there, keep striving, keep improving, and most importantly, guys—Don't ever give up!

I was walking up the fairway on #6 one day and I noticed something very strange on the green. There was a group of women in front of me putting on the green. I was waiting for them to finish when one of the women starting doing cartwheels—CARTWHEELS! Later, as the ladies were coming down the adjacent fairway on #8 and I was coming up the fairway on #7, we passed each other and I told this attractive, young lady that I appreciated her athleticism. She smiled and said she only did that when she made a birdie.

It's nice to see people happy like she was, especially women. It's harder for women to be happy than it is for men to be happy . . . don't you think? After all, men are such simple creatures, it doesn't take much to amuse us or keep us satisfied. Just look at the facts if you are a man:

> Your last name doesn't change.
> The garage is all yours.
> Wedding plans take care of themselves.
> You can never be pregnant.
> You can wear NO shirt to a water park.
> Car mechanics tell you the truth.
> The world is your urinal.
> You never have to drive to another gas station restroom because this one is too icky.
> Same work, more pay.
> Wrinkles add character.
> Wedding dress, $5,000. Tux rental, $100.
> People never stare at your chest when you're talking to them.
> One mood all the time.
> Phone conversations are over in 30 seconds flat.
> A five-day vacation requires only one suitcase.
> You can open all your own jars.
> Three pairs of shoes are more than enough.
> The same hairstyle lasts for years, even decades.
> You only have to shave your face and neck.
> You can "do" your nails with a pocket knife.
> And, you can do Christmas shopping for 25 relatives on December 24 in only 25 minutes.

***

Okay, we've finished hole #6 and we're one-third of the way around the course. We're also one-third of the way through our lives. Some of us are married, some of us have families, some of us have good jobs . . . and some of us don't have any of these. So what?

There's still plenty of time to do all of these things or just one or two of them—it's up to you. At this point in your life, it's possible to recycle yourself . . . or not. Did you know that six weeks after an aluminum can is recycled, it is back on the shelf in the form of a new can. You can do that as well. What's in the past is in the past. All that matters is what you do with what's ahead of you. Take Mick Jagger of the Rolling Stones as a good example (or bad example, depending on your viewpoint). Mick doesn't let age determine his actions. Rightly or wrongly, he pretty much does what he wants. Mick's youngest son is younger than one of his great-grandchildren. Think about that!

Or, you could go in the opposite direction and end up like your automobile, which spends 95% of its useful life parked. Don't be an automobile. Have the courage to begin without any guarantees of success. Be one of the few people who have the imagination for reality.

#7

Let me start this section by admitting that I don't like hole #7. Sorry, Lynn; sorry, Shannon. It's not a bad hole by any means; in fact, when I was a member here twenty years ago, I liked this hole. However, age has changed my opinion considerably. First of all, this hole is always into the wind—ALWAYS! Then, it's also uphill—ALWAYS. And, I'm much older than I used to be— ALWAYS. Combine those three qualities and they spell DISLIKE.

When I was younger, I could drive the ball up to the top of the hill and have a seven, eight, or nine iron into the green. Now . . . when I hit a good drive, into the wind, up the hill, I am still left with a three-iron, hybrid, or even a 3-wood into the green. Gribble was correct, for once in his life, when he told me, "Age always wins."

Then, when you finally arrive at the green, it's sloped extremely fast from back to front. If you are unlucky enough to hit your ball above the hole and have the misfortune of putting back down the hill, well . . . I'll say a prayer for you. You'll need it.

This hole is a good example of life itself: fairly easy when you're young and extremely hard when you're old—especially if you make bad decisions. When you're young, you can eat unhealthy junk, go out drinking three or four times a week, never exercise, and you'll still feel great. Try doing those things when you're old. Unless your name is Gam, you'll end up feeling bad, looking bad, and being bad. Gam is the exception.

When I was a member here about twenty years ago, Gam was the epitome of everything all the "bad boys" wanted to be. He played golf every day, he gambled on nearly every shot, he drank all the time, he ate whatever he wanted, he told the best and dirtiest jokes, and he chased all the pretty girls. But, we ain't Gam. We can't do that. If we did, we'd end up looking like Bill, or Gordon, or A.C., or God forbid, like me! Gam is an anomaly. Someone who is not really a live human being. He inhabits his body, he acts like a human, but there is no way in the world a REAL human being could do the things Gam does and still be living. No way!

I was walking up the fairway on #7 one day with my friend, Arthur, who is a Vietnam veteran by the way, and he said, "Gary, did you know that 997 soldiers were killed on their first day in Vietnam? And, 1,448 were killed on their scheduled last day?"

I did not know that and I wondered how Arthur knew that. Plus, why did he choose to tell me that, now, as we walked up this fairway for me to hit my second shot to the green with a 3-hybrid, when I used to hit this same shot, years ago, with an 8-iron. Was it because he sensed that I wanted to "kill" this hole? Or, was he just remembering a time long in the past that was hard to let go?

Either way, I started thinking about Arthur's statement: 997 young men killed on their first day in Vietnam. It's hard for me to comprehend that. Certainly, most of those young men were partying, dating, golfing, and having fun with their lives only a few months before. Even worse, think about those 1,448 young men who died on their last day in Vietnam. How tragic is that? And here I am complaining about trudging up a hill, into the wind, hitting a 3-hybrid instead of an 8-iron!

I stopped at my ball, still thinking about those young men who lost their lives on the last day of service in Vietnam, until I heard, "Hey!" I looked over at Arthur who had stopped and was waiting on me to hit my shot. "It's hot out here . . . hurry up."

I did not want to hurry up. My mind was still cluttered. But, because Arthur is my friend, I went ahead and hit my 3-hybrid fat, twenty yards short of the green. Thanks, Arthur! We walked up to the green and when we had both chipped up and were lining up our putts, Arthur said, "Did you know that veterinarians are three times more likely than the general public to have contemplated suicide?"

***

#7 . . . the perfect hole to illustrate the difference between young and old age. How life can seem so fitting at either twenty-five or seventy-five. We don't think about the differences, certainly not when we're young. Most of us never think of getting old and the changes age will make to our lives. We just hit 8-irons and keep on going.

I wish I could have been like William Gladstone, the Prime Minister of the United Kingdom in 1895. He started collecting books at a young age and by the time he was eighty-five years old he had a personal collection of over 32,000 books. When he realized he couldn't hit an 8-iron any longer, he personally wheelbarrowed his entire collection of books from his home to the town's library. He said he desired to "bring together books who had no readers with readers who had no books."

As Arthur and I finished up our putts on #7, we started walking over to the tee box for hole #8 and I remembered an odd piece of trivia I heard on the History Channel. It was now my turn to impress Arthur with some valuable information. I pulled my driver out from my bag, looked over at him, and said, "Arthur, there are an estimated three million wrecked ships at the bottom of the world's oceans, but fewer than 1% of the world's shipwrecks have ever been explored."

He pulled a club out of his bag, looked at me solemnly, and replied, "So?"

***

One day I actually hit a great drive on this hole and the wind was only medium hard, not hurricane velocity. Then, I hit my second shot low (not on purpose) which was what we call a "windcheater." It rolled onto the surface and settled all the way at the back of the green. Unfortunately for me, the pin was on the front of the green. But I had hit this green in regulation and was very proud of myself. My playing partner that day was my friend, Cameron; at least I think he's my friend.

Cameron and I had an unofficial contest as we walked from hole to hole which involved seeing who could remember the most sports and music history and who had done the most interesting trivial deeds. For instance, he could name all members of the Dodgers starting lineup in 1965, but I could name all the members of the Yankees starting lineup in 1961! Obviously, I won this matchup rather easily. Then, he said he was in London once and visited the Abbey Road Studios where The Beatles recorded their albums. Unfortunately for him, I had to tell the story of coming out of a subway station in London and actually seeing George Harrison getting out of a car and walking in the Abbey Road studios. Clearly, another win on my part.

Cameron was so flustered with my George story that he hit his shot to the green a little short and was about fifteen yards in front of the green, while I was on the green—albeit, a long way away and up the hill from the flag, but I was on the green. I knew I had him on the ropes now; I only had to seal the deal. But . . . he made a good chip up to the pin and only had about an 8-footer for par while I still had to putt my ball down that slippery slope.

It pains me to tell what happened next: I putted my ball down the hill, past the hole, and off the green. I left my next shot about four feet short and it took me two more shots to finally hole out for a double-bogey six! Cameron missed his par putt but tapped in for a bogey five. But isn't life like that?

You think you're in good shape. You're looking better than someone else. Then, before you know it, you double-bogey something. It's gonna happen, you can count on it. Life will take advantage of all your mishaps. Just keep on going, don't get discouraged, and don't stop trying. Old Cameron didn't say anything--he's too nice for that--but as we were walking off the green that day he asked, "Did I ever tell you about the Sandy Koufax autographed baseball I have?"

#8

The 8th hole at Maple Chase is a par 5 that can be reached in two . . . IF you hit two good shots. If you don't hit two good shots and reach the green or come close to the green, there is a stand of trees on your left, a creek in front of you, a sand trap before the green, and grassy mounds over to the right. I was playing this hole recently with my friend Warren, his lady friend, Shirley, and my friend Gary. I hit a terrible slice off the tee, across the cart path, way right of the trees. Everyone else hit nice shots and they were in the middle of the fairway. It was embarrassing for me to trudge across our fairway and go into the adjacent fairway to locate my ball while everyone else was in the ideal location.

They all hit up short of the green, in ideal position to chip up and have putts at birdie. Since I was on the far side of a stand of pine trees, they couldn't see me when I hit my second shot to the green—it was a good one! It hit a little short and rolled up about ten feet from the cup. They didn't see my shot until they walked up to the green and saw a golf ball sitting close to the pin. Warren said, "Someone left a ball on the green."

Shirley added, "It must have been that group in front of us."

My friend Gary continued, "Just pick it up, I'll get it to them at the turn."

They had just finished this conversation as I was walking up and Warren asked, "Where did your ball go?"

"Right there," I answered as I pointed to my ball.

Warren frowned at me, Shirley smiled at me, and Gary asked, "That's your ball?"

I nodded, then Warren asked, "That's your third shot, right?"

"Nope . . . second."

Gary said, "That was your second shot?"

"Yep."

Shirley raised her hand and gave me a high five. Warren continued to frown at me. Gary just stood there with a quizzical look on his face, like I'd done a magic trick he couldn't figure out. Sweet! It doesn't happen often, but when life is kind to you and you get results that weren't expected, you should enjoy them to the max. It doesn't happen often.

You think you've been working in anonymity and your company suddenly offers you a promotion. You hear from a close friend that the girl you've been lusting over would like to meet you. Your kid gets accepted into college. Your latest test results come back great from the doctor. We need to enjoy all the bonuses we get in life. As we age, it seems as though they come less frequently, so we should enjoy them even more.

#8 can also be a cruel hole, similar to life. A good drive down the middle will put you in great position to reach the green, just as graduating from college will put you in a great position to start your professional career. Then, you hit a nice second shot up close to the green on this par 5 hole. Or, get hired on by a nice, profitable company at a good starting pay rate. Things are looking good. Then comes the really difficult part: the third shot, the shot that will determine if you have a chance to par the hole, bogey the hole, or maybe even birdie the hole.

As in life, there are important decisions to make. Do I stay with my current company? Should I explore other opportunities? These questions are difficult to answer and can have lasting consequences. It's very hard to know what to do, which road to take. I have talked with several guys on the course who told me they started in one line of work and ended up doing something completely different. Some made the right decisions, others were not so fortunate.

I know a guy who always wanted to be a minister. He went to college and took all the right courses, got the right degrees, and landed in a nice church right after school. Apparently, he had made all the right decisions and was set for life. But it didn't turn out that way. He was always wanting more. He wanted a bigger church, more salary, more responsibility. He did move up the chain rather quickly, from smaller churches to larger ones, but at what price? Soon, his congregations were getting tired of having a preacher who was always looking to advance and move on.

His last church virtually kicked him out when they learned that he was secretly applying for other jobs. Then, his reputation began to filter around and his name became bad news. He couldn't find a church anywhere. He thought he would take a break for a while and let things settle down. That break has now lasted over twenty-five years. He goes from job-to-job now, working meaningless, minimum wage jobs, wondering what in the world happened?

You've hit a good drive, then hit a nice second shot, and you ask yourself, "Do I want to get greedy and shoot for the pin? Or, should I just hit the safe shot and go from there?"

I was playing this hole one day and had hit a decent second shot but I had pulled it a little left. If I aimed for the pin on my third shot I would have to come very close to some tree limbs hanging over the fairway. As I was standing there trying to figure out if I should try this risky shot or just hit into the middle of the green and play it safe, old Arthur walked up to me and said, "Did you know that more than 750 million chickens are killed each year for KFC?"

My complete train of thought was interrupted as I said, "What?"

Arthur answered, "Yeah, chickens outnumber humans by 8 to 1. We need that many to at least maintain the current levels of consumption by humans." Then he walked away, back toward his ball. My whole train of thought was corrupted.

When I looked back at my ball and the pin, I wondered, "What in the world am I thinking. I can't hit that shot!" So, I hit a nice safe shot into the middle of the green and made a boring par. When we finished the hole, I asked Arthur, "What was that deal about the chickens for, anyway?"

He took a sip from his water bottle, then said, "Gary, a person hears only what they understand."

***

#8 seems to be an easy hole. You're thinking to yourself, *I should birdie this hole.* And, *I can birdie this hole, if I hit a good drive, if I hit a good second shot, if I hit a good third shot, and if I make a good putt.* That's a lot of "ifs."

"If" I lived in Hawaii, I'd live in the state with the longest life expectancy, at over 82 years. "If" I was a seabird called the artic tern, I could live up to 34 years and travel up to 1.5 million miles. And, "If" I was an albatross, I could go years without landing. I could spend at least six years of my life flying over the ocean without ever touching the ground. But I'm not. I have to make hard decisions, tough decisions, and life-changing decisions, often without having any relevant information to help with the decision-making process.

#8 looks easy and it can be easy . . . *If* you make the right choices and execute them properly. Just like in life.

#9

Finally! Getting to the halfway point. Golf is often characterized as "the front nine" and "the back nine"; however, if you talk about life and ask people what they think the front nine of their life is, or where the back nine of their life starts, I bet you'd get many different answers. Would the front nine be your childhood and school years? Or, would it include your early married life and having children? Or, maybe your own personal front nine lasts until you retire? I guess all of these could apply, depending on how you see life and what your perspective is.

Or, is it just a number? If life expectancy is around 77 years (unless you live in Hawaii), then your front nine would be around 38 years. But the thing is, we don't know how long we'll live . . . only God knows that. Look at the list of rock stars who thought they'd live forever but who all died at the age of 27:

- Brian Jones, one of the founding members of the Rolling Stones along with Keith Richards and Mick Jagger, who drank too much, did drugs too much, and drown in his own swimming pool.

- Alan Wilson, a member of the blues-revival band, Canned Heat. He was the lead singer on their most popular songs: "Going up the Country" and "On the Road Again."

- Jimi Hendrix, the most popular and influential of them all. Not bad for a high school dropout who couldn't read music. Also, a man who joined the Army and made 26 jumps with the 101st Airborne Paratroopers, but died an unnecessary death due to mixing barbiturates with alcohol.

- Janis Joplin, one of the most famous and influential women singers in rock history. She didn't truly understand the effects and danger of heroin . . . until it was too late.

- Jim Morrison, mystic, poet, shaman, filmmaker, and oh, yes . . . lead singer of The Doors, one of the most popular groups in history. He died in his bathtub, under suspicious and cloudy circumstances, exactly two years to the day that Brian Jones died.

- Ron "Pigpen" McKernan, keyboardist, singer, and harmonica player for the band he helped form in San Francisco . . . The Grateful Dead.

- Peter Ham, singer, songwriter, and guitarist for Badfinger.

- Kurt Cobain, singer, songwriter, and founding member of the grunge rock band, Nirvana. As Nirvana became one of the most popular bands of the 90s, he started using more and more cocaine, until he finally took a shotgun and blew his brains out.

- Amy Winehouse, pop and jazz singer who couldn't cope with celebrity and her newfound popularity.

There are at least fifteen more on this list, who all died at the age of 27. I doubt any of these unfortunate souls thought that the front nine of their lives would be at 13 and that the end would be so early. That's the point . . . we never know.

***

#9 is not easy, but it's a fair hole if you hit good shots. There is a creek about a hundred yards in front of the tee, which shouldn't come in play—the key word being shouldn't. Then, there is out-of-bounds on the right, with a sand trap guarding the right side of the fairway and another trap farther down the left side of the fairway. Simple—all you have to do is hit the ball down the middle and you'll be fine.

The fairway is not the problem . . . the green is. There is a large, inviting, and deep sand trap on the right side of this green, which LOVES golf balls. There also are two smaller traps on the left side of the green. Obviously, you have no choice except to hit your shot into the middle of the green . . . easy!

But even if you avoid the out-of-bounds and the sand traps in the fairway, and avoid the inviting sand traps around the green, your problems are only beginning on this pretty little hole. Remember the sexy-looking girl in college that you lusted over for several months? She was hard to get to know, she was always with someone else, maybe you even thought she was too good for you. Then . . . you finally arranged a date with her and she turned out to be a maniac! Remember her? She is the epitome of the green on #9.

That green is located on a large hill that slopes the green dramatically from back to front. And I emphasize the word "dramatically." No matter where the pin is located, you must not, you CANNOT land your shot above this hole. Why? Because, if you do, then you'll be putting down this slippery slope with very little chance of stopping your ball anywhere near the hole. And, if you're to the left or right of the pin, then your putt will break left or right, anywhere from 6 to 12 feet.

I've heard more cuss words on this green than any other green on the course. But, it's not the green's fault. You know how it is. You know how it slopes. You KNOW you cannot be above the hole and leave yourself a downhill putt—you know that! Then why do you do it? Why do you date the girl that you KNOW is trouble? Why take the job that you KNOW will not last. Why do you invest in that stock that you KNOW is risky? Why, why, why?

Because we're hot and cold. Because we're greedy, eager, impatient, craving, desirous, devouring, gluttonous, insatiable, penurious, ravenous, and voracious—in other words, we're male human beings. My golfing friend, Terry, says we humans are exactly like the planet Mercury: 800 degrees Fahrenheit at its equator, but fields of ice at its North and South Poles.

A few months ago, I was playing with my friend Gordon and a couple of other guys, both less handsome than Gordon so they will remain nameless. Gordon was playing well and hitting most greens in regulation but he couldn't make a putt. He probably missed four or five short, makeable putts on the front nine. On each putt, he would talk to his ball as it was rolling toward the hole, saying, "Go in, go in, go in!" But his ball never listened to him . . . never. We came to hole #9 and Gordon hit a nice shot on the green, but he was above the hole. Not good!

He tenderly tapped his putt toward the hole but somehow it stopped before it reached the hole, about two-and-a-half feet away. How it stopped on that steep slope is one of the mysteries of nature. Most times, when we're playing with each other, and there is a putt of that short distance, we'll tell each other, "That's good, pick it up." But, since this was a downhill two-and-a-half footer, no one said a word. Gordon gave us all ample time to utter the phrase, "That's good," but we didn't. We knew how hard a downhill putt was on this hole.

Gordon marked his ball and we all finished up. After he had placed his ball back on the ground, he then reached down and picked it up again, bringing it directly in front of his face. He held that ball about 12" from his nose and said, "Don't you dare go in that hole!" We all started laughing so hard that one of the guys walked over and picked up Gordon's ball and threw it to him. See? Men do have feelings.

***

This ninth hole has a special memory for me . . . unfortunately, only for me, because no one else saw either of the shots I hit there. I was playing by myself on each of the two occasions. The first time was about 18 years ago, the second time only a few months ago. I took a golf sabbatical of nearly 17 years in between these two monumental events. What was so momentous?

On the first occasion, I hit my second shot on this hole about 155 yards up onto the green and it rolled into the cup for an eagle 2! It was late in the day, after work, nearing dusk, and there was no one around to see my magnificent shot—only me. But I saw it. I reveled in my glory, I praised my achievement to the golf gods . . . it was exquisite. Except, no one saw it. I got my ball from the cup and took it home to keep in a prominent place (where my wife couldn't see it). Unfortunately, since I was playing by myself, I was using a dirty, beat-up, old ball with cart path scratches all over it. But it was sweet that special day.

Over the 17 years that I was away from golf, I often thought of that day and that shot. There were other memories as well, but this one was special to me. After my long time away from golf,

I realized there isn't much time left to do the things I've always wanted to do. I have to do those things now! Not just golf things . . . but everything. And, so should you. If you want to go to Jamaica and hang out on the beach with the Rastas—GO! If you want to go to Scotland and play St. Andrews and drink the best whiskey in the world while wearing a kilt—GO! If you want to walk to the bottom of the Grand Canyon, or hike into the wilderness of Alaska, or go to Berlin and walk on Hitler's bunker, or visit Carmel and take a whale-watching boat into the ocean, or this or that, or anything . . . GO! Do it now. Don't wait.

So, I started playing golf again to fulfill one of my dreams. I learned quickly that playing golf when you're older is much more difficult than playing when you're younger. Much more! But, I'm persistent. I began playing most days by myself, mostly because I wasn't good enough to play with anyone else. I needed practice—a lot of practice. Each time I walked up the fairway on #9, I always remembered the day long ago when I made that shot. I could almost see it and feel it. What a wonderful memory.

Nowadays, it is very difficult for me to reach the green, or get anywhere near the green. It's a hard hole for us older people. Then, one day, as I was once more playing by myself, something magical happened. I hit a decent tee shot but I was still about 165 yards from the green (which is a long, long way when you're old). I took aim and hit the ball dead center. It started for the green then hit in the middle of the green and gently rolled down the slope and dropped into the cup. At first, I thought my eyes had deceived me. After all, I am pretty old. But, no, I was seeing clearly. My ball had disappeared into the cup AGAIN. After 18 years, I had done it again!

I looked around: There was no one behind me, no one in front of me, and no one in the chipping area off to the right to verify my miraculous shot. DANG!! I put the club back in my bag, tried to smooth out all the hairs on my arms that were standing straight up, and then started walking up toward the green. As I got about twenty yards from the green I noticed a guy up on the driving range, well beyond the hole, standing there looking at me. As I walked onto the green, he started clapping—all by himself.

Incredibly, he had witnessed my miracle shot. He was watching me because we sort of knew each other from around the practice areas and had played together once. Brad, which is his name, came over and congratulated me as all the hairs on my arms once again stood straight up. I picked up my ball from the cup and was happy to see that it was a fairly new ball this time. One I could proudly display in my house (as long as my wife doesn't see it).

Front Nine

Half the round is complete. If you played well, you're probably excited and ready to start the back nine and continue your good play. If you didn't have a good front, you may be in a bit of trouble because the back nine here at Maple Chase seems to be a little tougher than the front. Which is similar to our lives in several ways.

The front half of your life is usually pretty easy and fun; you normally don't have a lot of serious issues to deal with. It's the last half where things start to get harrowing. A lot of us get married and have kids. You have to start saving for college, your jobs become more stressful, your health starts acting up—it ain't easy getting older. Usually, through no fault of your own, you start gaining weight over the years. Before you know it, your pants don't fit anymore. You can't walk eighteen holes like you used to. And, mowing the lawn totally exhausts you now.

I remember the first time my weight started bothering me. I had a yearly physical checkup scheduled, so during the appointment, I told the doctor I wanted to lose some weight. The Doctor told me, "Don't eat anything fatty."

So, I said, "What, like ice cream and cookies?"

And, he said, "No, just don't eat anything, Fatty!"

He was not a nice doctor. But many times the world is not nice to us. It reveals the harsh truth in many ways: your wife (or husband) is not the person you thought they'd be; you seem stuck in a dead-end job; your first-born child doesn't seem interested in schooling or going to college. Your back starts to ache, your knees hurt, you can't sleep, you need glasses, etc., etc., etc. Life can be and will be very challenging at times. But do we stop after 9 holes and go home? No! We keep playing, we keep trudging up and down those hills on the back side. We keep fighting and trying as hard as we can to do our best, because, if we don't . . .

So, you call Shirley or Bing or Kay and order a snack and something to drink after the first nine holes. Refresh yourself, tell each other a good joke, and prepare for the back nine, which you know will not be easy.

The Back Nine

#10

As I was standing on the tee at #10, my playing partner, Tom, said, "The young couple living next to me made a sex tape . . . I mean they obviously don't know that yet." By the time I stopped laughing, I had nearly forgotten about how much this hole scares me.

From the tee box, the fairway goes extremely downhill, with a creek crossing the fairway at the bottom of the hill. This menacing little creek SHOULDN'T come into play . . . right? From the creek, the fairway then goes steeply uphill and flattens out a little as you near the green. Oh, yes, I almost forgot, the fairway also slants precipitously to the right. *Precipitously* is the only word I can use here without cussing; however, I think in ancient Greek, it is a cuss word.

So, to keep the ball in the fairway, you must hit your tee shot down the left side and HOPE it will stay in the fairway and not roll too far right into the high grass. If you're young, like Morgan or Brad or Kevin, then you don't have to worry too much about this slope to the right; you just hit over everything. But, for us older human beings, it's tough to navigate at times.

On numerous occasions our second shots to this par 4 hole are blind, meaning we can't see the green or even the top of the pin. This is the result of us not hitting our tee shots up the hill far enough. So, our second shot is uphill, with a side-hill lie, to a green you can't see. Now you understand why this hole scares me every time I play it.

However, the owner of our course, a very handsome, intelligent, savvy, world-traveled businessman named Lynn, helped us all out recently by removing a sand trap guarding this hole and replacing it with some hilly mounds of high grass. Thanks, Lynn. When you finally hit your ball onto the green, you quickly learn what the words sloping, undulating, rolling, and tricky mean. This green is all those . . . and more. From the fairway, it looks rather flat. If you are new to the course and are actually standing on the green, it still looks rather flat. Until you hit your putt.

It is an optical illusion, similar to that tourist attraction in the mountains with the house that seems like you're walking uphill and standing crooked in the house—on a flat floor! Experience will teach you that everything breaks to the right (as you're looking at the green from the fairway) and that everything breaks from the back to the front. Most of us will learn this the hard way. My first time playing this hole, I was lining up my putt when a guy known as "The Hammer" walked behind me and said softly, "It breaks to the right."

I was studying the line of my putt and was convinced there was no way in the world that this putt could go right. No way! In fact, I was fairly certain that it would probably go left several inches. So, I ignored The Hammer's advice and played for a break to the left. Guess what? Of course, The Hammer was correct and my ball broke way right and I was left several feet away from the hole. Some of us are hard-headed. I always listened to The Hammer after that.

I only wish I'd listened to people like The Hammer during my life. People who told me what to do. People who explained how things would work out. People who knew from past history. People who were more experienced and smarter than I was. But I didn't. I had to learn the hard way. Had to make the mistakes that they warned me about. Experience is the hardest kind of teacher. It gives you the test first and the lesson afterward. Dang!

You've probably witnessed this behavior in your own kids. You warn them, you advise them, you guide them, but still, they go their own way. Just like you did when you were young. However, sometimes you give advice or accept advice that does not apply to your situation. Like here on #10; if someone tells me to "Hit it up the left side over the hill." Great. Sounds wonderful! But just how do I do that? I can't hit the ball that far anymore. Your advice is exactly right—just not for me.

I love my daughter but college was never in her future. No matter how hard I tried to convince her, it was not going to happen. Everyone is their own person, and we can give them advice, counsel them, and lead them, but we are not them. Just as you did years ago, your kids will probably make their own decisions as well—some you agree with and some you don't. You can still tell them, "This putt is going to break to the right." But, until they actually hit that putt and see for themselves, they probably won't believe it. Right, Hammer?

***

I had recently completed this hole and bogeyed it, as I often do. I still get mad. I still think I should hit the ball the way I did twenty years ago. I love to dream. As I slammed my club into my bag and started to walk to the next tee, my playing partner, Warren, walked up to me and told me this story:

A woman was shopping at the local supermarket where she selected:

> *A half-gallon of 2% milk,*
> *A carton of eggs,*
> *A quart of orange juice,*
> *A head of lettuce,*
> *A 2 lb. can of coffee, and*
> *A 1 lb. package of bacon.*

As she was unloading the items on the conveyor belt to check out, a drunk standing behind her was watching. While the cashier was ringing up the purchases, the drunk calmly stated, "You must be single."

She was a bit startled by this proclamation but intrigued by the derelict's intuition since she was indeed single.

She looked at the six items on the belt and saw nothing particularly unusual about her selections that could have tipped off the drunk to her marital status. Curiosity getting the better of her, she said, "Well, you know what, you're absolutely right. But how on earth did you know that?"

The drunk replied, "Cause you're ugly."

By the time I arrived at the next tee, instead of still being mad about my bogey on #10, I was giggling over Warren's joke, which was the best advice I received all day.

#11

If you're walking, this hole is your last respite of the day. If you're riding in a cart, it doesn't make any difference, but if you're walking, it's the last hole you don't have to climb up a steep slope to hit your next shot. Oh, it still has hills. The fairway slopes greatly from left to right and then about halfway to the hole, the entire fairway goes steeply downhill toward the green. But, no UPHILL walks. Remember this fact dearly as you're cursing the hills on the rest of the back nine.

This is what makes Maple Chase the great course it is: the front nine and the back nine are so different. No two holes are similar and each one presents its own set of difficulties and opportunities. Just as in life: Life in your 30's is different from life in your 40's, and from your 50's, and much different from life in your 60's or 70's. Trust me!

I played this hole one day with my friend, Mikey, who by the way, is so ugly that when he opens the door on Halloween, the kids give HIM candy. Anyway, he sliced his tee ball into the high grass and we never found it. Then he topped his next shot and it rolled about halfway down the hill. He chunked his next shot, then finally got on the green and promptly three-putted for an inglorious quadruple bogey. But instead of cussing and throwing his club, like some unnamed people I know, he just smiled and started walking off the green.

I said, "Dude, why in the world are you smiling at that mess you just made?"

He answered, "Cause I didn't have to walk UP a single hill to do it."

In my opinion, the green on this hole is the most difficult green to read on the whole course. There are absolutely no flat spots on the entire surface. There are mounds and hills and valleys and unseen magnetic forces that somehow pull your ball away from its intended target. Reminds me a lot of my early work career when I thought I was doing good but got passed over for promotion for someone who didn't deserve it (in my opinion).

Or, when your kid was playing Little League and the coach pulled him out of the game in the third inning and put in some dud in his place. Or, when you studied the stock market carefully, read all the financial patterns, and was certain that a particular stock or fund would accelerate—but it didn't. Life is like that; you just never know what's going to happen. You can study the green, read all the nuances, and still be fooled by unseen contours.

I know a lady, very attractive, smart, highly educated, successful, and one of the best people in town. She had been married over thirty years and thought everything was perfect, until it wasn't. One fateful day, her husband told her, "I don't love you. In fact, I've never loved you. I'm leaving." And he walked out. After thirty-some years, don't you think she had read him properly? She probably thought she knew everything there was to know. Until she didn't.

The good news is that she has recently remarried to a great and kind man and seems happier than we've ever seen her before. It's hard to read the green on #11 ... almost impossible. Just as it is trying to read people—you just never know.

In the United States, about 18,000 people have been successfully hidden by the witness protection program. This means each of our states on average has 300-400 of these people living with us. Maybe some are your friends. Maybe some are your golfing buddies. And, maybe I should pay closer attention to old Arthur from now on. He may be 83 years old, but that only enhances the odds of him being a shady, witness-protected, alien. Or not.

The point is, it's hard to know people. It's difficult to know what they really think, what they really want, who they really are. I could study the green on #11 all day and still misread it. The same with people. Sometimes, you just have to trust your instincts and intuitions and hope you don't get hurt too much. However, the good news is that sometimes you read the green just perfectly and your putt rolls into the cup, dead center. Yes!

***

From the tee area on #11 and down the fairway, it's possible to look back and see several holes on the front nine that you just finished playing. This overlook is very nice and especially scenic when everything is green and blooming. It's nice to look back and remember the good times, isn't it? Especially when you're getting older, sitting around with friends or relatives and remembering the fun times, the travels, the laughs. Not many of us remember chunking one in the lake on #6, or slicing one in the woods on #3, or dumping one in the creek on #4 ... no, we'd much prefer to remember the good shots.

Lots of times, walking around the course with golf partners, I'll remember strange things my playing buddies told me. I don't know why they say the things they do ... maybe the hills have worn them out and their minds aren't functioning rationally, or maybe they just like to ruminate. As with my friend, Roland, who told me once that Michigan, which borders no ocean, has more lighthouses than any other state. I asked him how he knew this and he answered, "Because that's where I'm from." I didn't know Roland was from Michigan, and while I was thinking about that, he continued, "And the Great Lakes contain 21% of the world's surface freshwater." Roland was very proud of that fact. Why, I don't know, but he was.

Another day, I was walking up the fairway on #7 and a small jet passed overhead, which isn't unusual since our course is located near Winston-Salem's regional airport. My buddy, Ben, stopped and looked up at the plane as it passed over us, then asked me, "Gary, have you ever wondered how many planes are in the air at any given time?"

I stopped my golf cart and looked over at Ben and answered truthfully, "No."

He continued, "Well, there is an average of 9,728 planes carrying over 1.2 million passengers in the sky at any given time." I nodded to show Ben that I understood him, then he finished by saying, "Yep." We finished the hole in silence and started walking up to the next tee and Ben added, "And, did you know that Canada has more lakes than the rest of the world combined?"

"No, I didn't know that, Ben."

"It's true."

I nodded, then asked Ben, "Are you from Canada?"

"Nope, but it's true."

I love golf.

#12

Doce--the twelfth hole . . . or, as many have described it: tenacious, malicious, inflexible, rugged, unyielding, dreadful, and intimidating. You can also add to this list every four-letter word you've ever heard your dad scream out when he hit his thumb with a hammer. That's #12.

Here's a fact: In the two days following a Daylight Savings Time switch-over, there's an 8% increase in the rate of strokes.

Here's another fact: If you walk up the hill on #12 you have a 99% chance of cursing this hole, cursing golf, cursing Jerry, and cursing yourself for not renting a cart.

Remember when you finally figured out your profession and had a good feeling that you were on the right track? Then, suddenly, everything became hard. The business didn't seem as promising as it did earlier, your future didn't seem as rosy. The road to success seemed uphill, curvy, murky, and fraught with all sorts of dangers. Nobody told you it was going to be this hard. Nobody told you the road to success was up this steep of a hill. Then, you remembered something your granddaddy once told you, "Everything is hard before it's easy."

So, you keep working, you keep trudging up that hill, never giving up, one step after another. Is it easy? No! Is it worth all this effort? Let's hope so. Just like the hike up #12, it ain't no fun, it wears you out, it's not fair . . . but, you can't go forward until you complete this ordeal. My playing partner Ben birdied this monster of a hole two times in a row—I witnessed it. Of course, on his next round, he double-bogeyed, but hey, he's only human.

Another factor about this hole is that you must use at least two or three additional clubs to reach the green. If you would normally hit an 8-iron, then you will probably have to use a 6-iron, or maybe even a 5-iron up this steep slope. Plus, the green is tightly bordered on the right-hand side by some thick woods with sticky undergrowth and there is a menacing sand trap to the left of the green.

When you finally do reach the putting surface, your adventure is just beginning. The green itself slopes from back to front pretty significantly. If you're putting downhill, it's very easy to putt the ball off the green and watch it roll down the slope of the fairway a good twenty or thirty yards. It's cruel, in a golf sense, not in reality.

As I'm writing this, today's date is June 6. Some of us remember this date; younger people probably don't. My uncle remembered it very well. He was one of the chosen to parachute behind German lines on D-Day, June 6, 1944. He only spoke of this day one time that I'm aware of. He said they left before dawn and jumped from the airplane in complete darkness. They couldn't see anything, including the ground, until they landed. Some guys fell in trees and broke limbs, some fell on houses, some fell in lakes and streams and were killed instantly.

He landed abruptly in a field and made his way to some trees for cover. It was still pitch black and the armies from both sides were all firing shots at each other. According to my uncle, he didn't know where he was, where the enemy was, or where his buddies were—everyone was shooting blindly. He did have a compass and knew he was supposed to go back west toward the Normandy beaches to meet the Allied forces.

All the Allied troops were given little clickers to use on the ground. They would make this "clicking" sound so the American soldiers would know when they heard this sound, that it was one of their buddies. However, as many soldiers were killed, the Germans took those clickers from the fallen Americans and now EVERYONE was making "clicking" sounds.

He finally made his way back to the beaches after the sun had risen and saw the sight that has haunted him for over fifty years: On the beach, the Americans had piled up the bodies of their dead comrades, like cordwood, to await transport off the beach. For over fifty years, whenever he closed his eyes, that's what he saw—the bodies of his buddies, those brave young men, twenty and twenty-one years old, piled up like cordwood on the beaches at Normandy.

I guess trudging up that hill on #12 isn't so hard after all.

***

Shannon and Lynn have been kind enough to place a bench on the tee at #13, so we older people, who have just trudged up the long hill on #12, can rest a few minutes and catch our breath. We were sitting there recently when the cart girl, who rides around the course with cold drinks and snacks, rode up near us. This day, it was Kay, a lovely young lady, who stopped and asked if we needed anything. I had forgotten to bring a snack with me, so I thought I'd better get something to keep my energy up for the last several holes. I walked over to her cart and noticed there was a small sign on the cart that read, "Lobster Tails: $2.00"

Wow! That sounded great. I handed her the two dollars and said, "I'll have one, please."

She smiled and replied, "Once upon a time there was this lobster . . . "

***

One other day, I had finished my round, after playing by myself, and had stopped at the clubhouse to sit outside in one of the comfortable rocking chairs to have a cold drink while I cooled off and let my shirt dry out. Two chairs down from me sat a man about my age who also looked like he had just finished playing. I smiled and asked how he was doing. He answered, "I was okay until I climbed up that hill on #12. That wore me out."

We both laughed and introduced ourselves. His name was John. I had never seen John before and I've never seen him since that day; however, I'm sure glad I met him when I did. I'm a curious sort of guy and I always ask a bunch of questions, like: Did you grow up around here? Where did you go to school? How many kids do you have? Etc., etc., etc. Old John was fascinating.

He grew up in Indiana and was a very good high school basketball player. He played in the same conference as one of the N.C. State great players—Monte Towe. Then, through a series of events, he ended up attending Stanford University and playing basketball for them. I was in awe of his stories, especially when he was telling me about playing against UCLA and the great Bill Walton. I could hardly believe I was sitting there talking to a guy who played against one of the greatest college basketball players ever. All because he and I both walked up #12 and were tired and needed to sit and rest. So, in retrospect, #12 isn't so bad after all. John, I loved talking to you that day and I hope to see you again soon.

#13

After #12, everything is good . . . you're happy to still be breathing, you're laughing and telling jokes with your friends, and life is groovy. One day, as we were sitting on the bench at #13 waiting to tee off, my friend David told me this story:

Three golfing buddies died in an auto accident and went to heaven. Upon arrival, they noticed the most beautiful golf course they have ever seen. St. Peter told them they were welcome to play the course, but he cautioned them with one rule: "Don't step on the ducks."

The men had blank expressions on their faces, and finally one of them said, "The ducks?"

"Yes," St. Peter said. "There are millions of ducks walking around the golf course, and when one of them is stepped on, he squawks, and then the one next to him squawks, and soon they're all raising hell and it really breaks the tranquility. If you step on the ducks, you'll be punished."

The men start playing the course, and within 15 minutes one of the guys stepped on a duck. The duck squawked, and soon there was a deafening roar of ducks quacking. St. Peter appeared with an extremely homely woman and asked, "Who stepped on a duck?"

"I did," admitted one of the men.

St. Peter immediately pulled out a pair of handcuffs and cuffed the man to the homely woman. "I told you not to step on the ducks," he said. "Now you'll be handcuffed together for eternity."

The two other men were very cautious not to step on any ducks, but a couple of weeks later, one of them accidentally did. The quacks were as deafening as before, and within minutes, St. Peter walked up with a woman who was even uglier than the other one. He determined who stepped on the duck by seeing the fear in the man's face, and he cuffed him to the woman. "I told you not to step on the ducks," St. Peter said. "Now you'll be handcuffed together for eternity."

The third man was extremely careful. Some days he wouldn't even move for fear of nudging a duck. After three months of this, he still hadn't stepped on a duck. St. Peter walked up to the man and had with him the most beautiful woman the man had ever seen. St. Peter smiled and, without a word, handcuffed him to the beautiful woman and walked off.

The man, knowing that he would be handcuffed to this woman for eternity, let out a sigh and said, "What have I done to deserve this?"

The woman replied: "I don't know about you, but I stepped on a duck."

***

Hole #13 is an interesting hole. It's a short par 4 that many of the long-hitters can reach with their drives. I've come close several times, in my younger years, but I've never actually made the surface of the green. I've even heard stories of some long-hitters who intentionally hit their ball OVER the green because it's easier to chip back onto the green from that direction. I would never know.

Of course, there is some danger with this little hole that you must be aware of. The left side of the fairway is lined with tall, thick grass and weeds—nearly impossible to find your ball in that mess, much less hit out of it. On the right-hand side is a sand trap with a thick stand of woods beyond that. To top it all off, the green itself slopes distinctly to the left, but you can't be too careful because there are sand traps on the right side and left side of the green. So . . . it may be a short little hole, but it will bite you good if you're not careful. Instead of trying to drive the green, and opening yourself up to all sorts of danger, I've always found the smart play, for me, is to simply hit a shot into the middle of the fairway and leave myself a short wedge shot to the green.

Examples of this hole in real life are:
1. When you're young and burning with extra testosterone and you go full throttle for the hot, young girl who's driving all the boys crazy. You absolutely don't think of the tall weeds to the left, or the sand trap and woods on the right . . . all you see is that open, inviting, welcoming green. And, you go for it! She's worth it! Right?
2. Your friends have told you about a stock that is getting ready to "skyrocket!" You believe them. They're smart guys. They're always right. You take your savings and cash in some of your other stuff and you buy it. You are going to be RICH! Only . . .
3. You're doing well with your career, things are on track, but one of your friends seems to be doing a LOT better than you are. One day he tells you he could probably get you on with his company and you could be successful just like him. So, without thinking, you quit your good, stable job with benefits, pension, security, and promise for the quick solution of fast, easy money. Does it work out in the long run? For your sake, I hope so.

There are untold other examples of how we all do things like this—looking for glory instead of taking the safe, secure route. Especially with us men . . . sometimes we can be especially reckless, foolish, and crazy. Women are much more stable, and prettier, and smarter, and better than us. Right? Women would never improve their lie in the rough, would they? Women would never drop a ball in a better position; they'd never "find" their ball in the trees when no one else could. Nah, women would never do those things. But we would.

Would we ever think of cheating at anything OFF the golf course? Probably not . . . maybe . . . nah, we wouldn't. But on the golf course? Don't lie and tell me you never have! Ahh, we're just playing for fun; what difference does it make?

Really . . . what difference does it make? No one will ever know. 99% chance I'll never be noticed. Of course, the black widow spider's bite only has a 1% chance of fatality, but what if you are in that 1%? In China, if you're caught cheating on a college exam, the maximum penalty is 7 years in prison! And, 27,000 trees are cut down EVERY day just to make toilet paper. Hard to believe! Right, and what difference does it make if I've gone way off course here? Or, if you mark down a 4 when you really made a 5. Who's gonna know?

I'll tell you who'll know. Somebody decent. Somebody honorable. Somebody you trust. Somebody you love. Or, maybe even somebody like our ex-President Harry S. Truman. Mr. Truman was a different kind of president, unlike those we've witnessed recently. He probably made as many, or more, important decisions regarding our nation's history as any of the other 32 Presidents preceding him; however, a measure of his greatness may rest on what he did after he left the White House.

The only asset he had when he died was the house he lived in, which was in Independence, Missouri. His wife had inherited the house from her mother and father and that's where they lived their entire lives, except for the years in the White House.

When he retired from office in 1952 his income was a U.S. Army pension reported to have been $13,502 a year. That's all. No book deals. No worldwide speaking engagements. No television specials. Nothing but the $13,502 from his Army pension. When Congress found out that he was paying for his own postage stamps and personally licking them, they granted him an "allowance" and later upped his pension to $25,000 a year.

Now think about the following facts for a minute or two and see if they could be applied to any of our recent Presidents. After President Eisenhower was inaugurated, Harry and his wife Bess drove their car home to Missouri, from Washington, D.C., by themselves. They had no Secret Service following them. And, when he was President, he paid for all of his own travel expenses and his own food. When he was offered corporate positions at large salaries, he declined, stating, "You don't want me. You want the Office of the President, and that doesn't belong to me. It belongs to the American people and it's not for sale." (Not for sale? Really? . . . Biden, Trump, Obama, Bush, Clinton, etc., etc., etc.?)

Modern politicians have found a new level of success in cashing in on the Presidency, resulting in untold wealth. Today, too many in Congress also have found a way to become quite wealthy while enjoying the fruits of their offices. Harry should be here to teach them all a valuable lesson: political offices are not for sale.

Good old Harry Truman was correct when he observed, "My choices in life were either to be a piano player in a whore house or a politician. And to tell the truth, there's hardly any difference!"

I wish we could clone him.

***

Back to Maple Chase . . . I started this 13th hole with a story, so I'll end it with a story about people my age:

An elderly couple has dinner at another couple's house, and after eating, the wives leave the table and go into the kitchen. The two gentlemen were talking, and one says, "Last night we went out to a new restaurant and it was really great. I would recommend it very highly."

The other man asks, "What is the name of the restaurant?"

The first man thinks and thinks and finally asks, "What is the name of that flower you give to someone you love? You know... The one that's red and has thorns.'"

"Do you mean a rose?"

"Yes, that's the one," replied the man. He then turns towards the kitchen and yells, "Rose, what's the name of that restaurant we went to last night?"

#14

Only five holes left to play. You're starting down the backstretch of the course . . . and your life. Has each of them been good to you? Are you close to par? Have your plans worked out at home? Are you happily married? Are your kids on the right track? Is your job progressing well? Have you started saving adequately for retirement? Thousands of questions you're probably asking yourself right now. It can be a daunting task trying to answer all these questions . . . daunting and frightening.

Hole #14 is a long par 5 that goes down a long slope, then back up quickly to the green. A stand of thick trees lines the right-hand side of the fairway all the way to the hole and a stretch of high-grass lines the left-hand side of the fairway. But, the fairway itself is pretty wide and gives you a good target. One of the problems lies in the fact that at one point the fairway slopes precipitously downhill. So, you'll probably have a downhill lie hitting to an uphill green—that's not easy.

But when is life ever easy? Business ventures go south, the stock market is volatile, your health is unknown at times, and who knows if your kids will ever figure it out? Sometimes it feels as though your entire life is going downhill and the finish line is WAY uphill. There are times when you simply don't know if it's worth the effort any longer . . . when you may feel like you're done. Almost to the point of giving up. Don't! Weird, wonderful, miraculous things can happen in an instant that can change your life. You just never know.

An example: A couple of years ago my friend Warren was playing in a tournament at our club for the Senior Club Championship. It was a 36-hole event and by the last hole the tournament was virtually over because one guy had a two-shot lead coming to this last hole, a par-5. This guy in the lead was not Warren; it was his playing partner in the last group of the day. I'm sure Warren thought his chances of anything except a second-place finish were only dreams. Did he give up? No, he gave it his best.

His playing partner, whom I won't name because these events are too painful, even today, teed off first and pulled his tee shot into some rough on the left side of this fairway. Warren hit a great drive right down the middle. The guy with the two shot lead played it safe and did the smart thing by punching his shot out into the fairway—after all, he had a two shot lead. Then, he hit his third shot up near the green but still not on the green.

Warren started thinking, *"If I can hit my second shot onto the green here, I could two-putt for a birdie, and if the guy in the lead bogeys, then we'll be tied!"* He still had nearly two hundred yards to the green, which is a very tough shot for most of us seniors. He lined it up and made a beautiful swing and the ball started sailing directly for the green. Warren started thinking, *"It's got a chance."* Then, as the ball started coming down, he thought, *"This is gonna be good!"* He watched as the ball bounced, then rolled directly at the pin. Then, he saw his ball HIT the pin and stop 18" away! It was an amazing shot with incredible results. He was only a tap-in putt away from an eagle 3.

Of course, his playing partner also saw this magnificent shot and became momentarily flustered . . . who wouldn't have? Unfortunately, he skulled his next shot over the green, then chipped back onto the green, and unfortunately two-putted for a tragic double-bogey 7. This fellow went from a two-shot lead on the last hole to suddenly losing by 2 shots.

When Warren was standing on that last tee, two shots behind, do you think he EVER thought he'd end up winning by two shots? Probably not. But, he gave it his best, never stopped trying, and was lucky enough to be on the winning side of a miraculous story.

***

The green on this hole, #14, is a two-tiered putting surface. There is a fairly level area up at the top of the hill and a curvy area down at the bottom of this green. Both are equally hard to putt. I've had six-foot putts at the bottom area that will break four feet from left-to-right—it's that tough. One of the best features of this green is that there's a bathroom just off the playing area to the right. When you're old, that is important!

It's a nice, solid, sturdy, cement bathroom which saves a lot of us from some pretty unpleasant moments . . . right Bill? One day, as Bill made his required trip to the restroom, my mind started wondering, as we were waiting on him to perform his daily ritual. I had read somewhere that China used more cement between the years 2011 & 2013 than the United States used the entire 20th century!

When Bill finally emerged from his "second home," I told him this valuable piece of information and he said, "So what? The biggest state in the country, Alaska, has less than 5,000 miles of paved public roads."

So, I countered with, "But, did you know that there are more than 25,000 islands in the Pacific Ocean?"

He stared intently at me for a few seconds, then turned to look back at the bathroom he just came from and said, "I wouldn't go in there if I were you."

***

One hot, humid, summer day, I was walking down this long fairway with Arthur, when a jet, which had just taken off from the airport close to us, flew directly overhead. I looked up at it, but Arthur stopped his cart and stood, staring at the jet as it flew on past us. I wondered what thoughts must be going through his 83-year-old mind. Was he remembering his days as a sharecropper in the rural south? Maybe he was thinking of his career in the Air Force, with a time spent in Vietnam. Or perhaps remembering a trip he took one time with his wife who had recently died.

When he started walking again, I went up to him and asked, "What were you thinking about back there?"

He looked at me, smiled, and answered, "Nothing."

I didn't believe him. But I knew enough to let it go, to let him reminisce on whatever special thoughts he was having . . . I understood. So, I let him walk on a bit by himself, then just to get his mind thinking of something else, I walked up and asked him, "Arthur, which of the fifty United States is closest to Africa?"

He nodded, then looked at me, then stared at the ground, then frowned, and finally answered, "Florida."

It isn't Florida; the correct answer is Maine. But I just nodded back at him and smiled. He asked, "Right?"

I said, "When are you ever wrong?"

He smiled and started humming an old Otis Redding song about sitting on the dock of a bay somewhere. Life is good.

#15

This 15th hole is the shortest hole on the course . . . and maybe the most dangerous. It's a par 3 over a sizeable lake, which is dangerous for sure; however, in my opinion, it is the slope of the green which makes it so scary. It tilts severely from the far end, up top, down to the low end of the green, next to the lake. And, if you somehow miss the green, as we all do, the fairway on each side of the green also slopes severely down to the water. It's not uncommon to see tee shots miss the green left or right, and then roll back down into the lake. I've heard many new cuss words on this hole--words that I never knew existed.

I was standing on the tee recently, waiting to settle my nerves so I could hit my ball over this lake, probably taking a little too long, when my playing partner, Roger, asked, "Everything okay?"

"Yeah," I answered. "I was just thinking from my past experience that I can't take a chance on being short here and ending up in the lake."

Roger nodded and said, "Experience is what you get when you don't get what you want."

That sounded very profound . . . I wasn't exactly sure what it meant, but it sounded good, so I hit my ball over the lake and almost on the green. Thanks, Roger. As I was walking over to my ball, I thought to myself, *"I have to be more positive on the course, when facing shots like that."* Then, I remembered a Positive Thinking course I took in graduate school . . . it was crap—I knew it would be.

This little hole can definitely play on your mind. The shortest hole on the course, but one filled with danger, one that requires solid contact and no indecision. But still, a lot of us will switch and use an "old ball" off the tee . . . just in case. Many, many times in my life, I've known the right thing to do. I've known what decisions to make, I've known the choices and actions that are required, but still . . . it's so hard to commit to doing those things.

Little things, like eating healthy, limiting your alcohol consumption, exercising more, saving a little more, treating your spouse a little better, being nicer . . . I know I can do it; you know you can do it. I know we can.

***

I was recently playing this hole with my old friend, Bill, who hit a bad shot and dumped his ball into the lake. He was not happy! But, being the good Moravian elder that he is, he didn't utter any cuss words (that I could hear). We walked over to the drop area where people who have hit balls in the lake are required to play from. He took the new ball from his pocket and dropped it on the ground. Then, he hit a nice-looking shot up to the top of the green and it almost stopped, but then, gravity started working.

His ball started creeping, ever so slowly, down the hill toward the pin at the bottom. I honestly thought his ball had no chance of rolling all the way down the hill—but it did. It kept slowly turning, almost as if in slow motion, until it rolled and hit the pin and dropped into the cup. Almost a hole-in-one—if he hadn't hit his first ball in the water. But he did hit his first ball in the water—and, he recovered to make a par.

If you lose your dream job, can you recover to find a better job? If your spouse leaves you, for whatever reason, can you recover and find a better partner? If your investments go south, can you recover and stay on track? If one of your kids drops out of college, can you still support them and lend them the encouragement they need to get back on track? If you get a bad diagnosis from the doctor, can you recover? Life is hard. There will be setbacks. We'll all hit balls in the water. The important issue is, can you recover and keep going? Yes . . . you can. Just like old Bill, who holed out his penalty shot. You can too. Just don't give up.

***

My favorite thing about this little hole is all the different kinds of birds who live around the lake. Of course, we have the ever-present geese, which are all over the course—apparently, they really like to congregate here because of the size of the lake and the lush grass around the edges. At some point in time, someone suggested we get a couple of swans to move into the lake. That person said that swans and geese don't like each other and maybe the geese would leave. Not so. I see them resting together, eating together, sleeping together, and swimming together.

Then, there are the dive-bombing ducks that swoop in at head-level to skim across the lake before stopping. Several times, they have come in so low that I felt as though I could have reached up and grabbed one. Certainly, I could have zonked one with my sand wedge if I was as accurate as Paul or Kevin or Randy. But I'm not. I just like to see them circle the lake, then swoop in low and skim across the water. Geese, ducks, and swans, all together . . . pretty cool.

One fortunate day for me, I was lucky enough to play nine holes with a sixteen-year-old young lady who is on the Reagan High School golf team. This young lady is extremely good—with the emphasis on "extremely." Even more so, she is a better person than golfer; her parents have done an outstanding job in teaching her life lessons, manners, and respectability. She didn't laugh at all when I hit a bad shot. For the nine holes I played with her, she was under par and never hit anything close to a bad shot. But, the best part of that day, for me, was listening to her talk and tell stories of things that happened to her in tournaments, and things other girls have done trying to gain an advantage when playing against her.

She was quiet at first and never really opened up until we got to this little par 3 hole with the lake. While we waited on the tee for the green to clear in front of us, she told me of a class she was taking in high school that was defining the differences and similarities in some of the world's governments. She said she didn't quite understand what made socialism different from democracy, and what made those different from something like communism. This was during an election year and all those terms were in the news every day—for me, it was tiring and burdensome hearing that junk on the news all the time.

She asked if I understood all these forms of government, because she didn't. So, I tried to make it as easy as possible to explain, especially in golf terms. I said, "Here's an easy way to remember the differences in each of them:

Socialism: you have two new Titleist golf balls, you give one to your playing partner.

Communism: you have two new Titleist golf balls, you give both new balls to Maple Chase and they may let you use a practice range golf ball if you need one.

Fascism: you have two new Titleist golf balls, which you give to Maple Chase, and Maple Chase sells them and keeps the money.

Nazism: you have two new Titleist golf balls. Maple Chase shoots you and keeps the golf balls.

Anarchism: you have two new Titleist golf balls. You keep both your golf balls, then break in the clubhouse and steal 12 more new Titleist golf balls.

Capitalism: you have two new Titleist golf balls. You sell one of your Titleist balls, then buy a dozen new Callaway golf balls with your earnings.

She kept nodding her head as if she understood this nonsense until I mentioned the last part about the Callaway golf balls. She was playing Callaways, her favorite ball. So, she just quietly went ahead and hit her Callaway Chrome Soft golf ball onto the green about eight feet away from the hole and made a birdie. Everything is so much easier when you're young.

#16

I started to omit this hole from my course description. I hope I can be impartial when I describe how unfair, cruel, immoral, unethical, unwarranted, dishonorable, grievous, shameless, unscrupulous, vile, wicked, and illegal this hole really is. Well . . . in all fairness, maybe it's not illegal. But it should be! On every course in the world (except in Ireland) there will be one hole that just doesn't suit you. One hole that simply irks your bones and makes you want to curse before you've even hit a shot. For me, this is that hole.

I'm going to try to be as fair as I can (which will be difficult) as I attempt to give an accurate and unbiased description of this evil hole (if that is possible) since that is my duty in documenting these events. Okay, here I go. This evil par 4 hole is lined with trees on both sides. On the left-hand side of the fairway, these trees are thick, gloomy, dark, dangerous, haunting, and frightening. That's not so much the case on the right-hand side; however, the entire fairway slopes precipitously to the left, toward this foreboding forest. I've experienced great injustice and even immoral activity on this hole when I hit my tee shots.

If I hit a shot down the left side of the fairway, it is automatically in the trees to the left. If I hit a drive down the middle of the fairway, the slope will turn it left and I will once again be in the trees. There is an alley about 10 yards wide down the right-hand side of the fairway to hit your drive. If you are fortunate enough to find this alley, you MIGHT be lucky enough to avoid the trees. But . . . if you hit too far right, then you are in the trees on the right-hand side of the fairway. What's a good old southern Baptist boy to do?

And if you think the fairway slopes severely to the left, wait till you see the green! Everything goes left! Way left. Left of Bernie Sanders, left of Al Gore, AOC, Castro, Ilhan Omar, and even left of Lenin and Marx! There, I think that's a fair, unbiased description.

Plus, I almost forgot . . . from the tee area, the fairway goes severely downhill to the bottom, then curves substantially uphill toward the green, and always slopes to the left—always to the left. You are either hitting from a downhill lie to an uphill green, or from a sidehill lie, with the ball about 18" above your feet. Heck, Phil Mickelson couldn't hit those shots when he was young and crazy and stupid, and certainly not now, when he's old and crazy and stupid.

***

When I first joined the golf club, I met Roger pretty early on and started playing with him. He seemed nice and friendly and I felt as though I could trust him. Until . . .

We had just come to this hole #16 and things were going great, at least for me. Roger was having some trouble with his swing; it was a little off. We hit our tee balls and he didn't hit a particularly good shot, and he was telling me the trouble he was having as we were walking down the steep hill of this fairway. We were both walking and pushing our golf carts as I was listening to Roger's description of his swing problem.

I had just purchased my new push cart; it was a nice one and I was proud of it. I was also wearing new golf shoes that I bought when I recently joined the club and a new pair of golf shorts— I was looking good! As we got about three-fourths of the way down this hill, Roger stopped his cart, put the brake on, started taking a few practice swings, and said, "I think my elbow is flying out too far. Can you see anything?"

I also stopped to look at his swing, though it was very doubtful I could tell him anything helpful. I turned my cart sideways so it wouldn't roll down the hill, but I didn't put the brake on. Then, I turned to look at Roger as he practiced his swing. After his follow through, he pointed at me. I didn't know why he was pointing; then he shouted at me, "Look!"

I was looking; I didn't know what else he wanted me to do. But he wasn't pointing at me at all. He was pointing at my golf cart, which had somehow succumbed to the effects of gravity and had started rolling down the hill by itself. By the time I turned around and saw it, it was at least twenty yards ahead of me and barreling toward the bottom of the hill, over to the left, where the creek is. I started running after it--well, as fast as an old man can run-- but I wasn't too worried.

My cart was headed directly for the creek alright, but this creek was surrounded by dense woods and thick undergrowth. I knew my cart would be stopped by some tree or shrub or bush. It might have a scratch or something, but that was all. Then, as I started to slow my so-called run, I noticed it: a small opening in the trees about three feet wide. This opening was still twenty-five yards ahead of the path my cart was on. I honestly thought there was no way on God's earth that my cart, rumbling uncontrollably down this hill, could possibly fit in that one small opening in these dense woods. I was wrong!

My cart went through that tiny opening as if it was guided by magic, or Elon Musk, and then hit a stump, flipped up in the air, and splashed into this murky creek. By the time I arrived at the scene, with Roger close behind me, my cart, my golf bag (with my wallet, my phone, my keys, my medicine, and my new golf towel) were totally immersed in this brown, gooey, murky mess.

If I hadn't actually seen it go in, I would never have known it was in there. Totally underwater and hidden from view. I couldn't believe what had just happened. I looked at Roger and he looked back at me and said, "Did you see anything wrong with my swing?"

I edged close to the water but still couldn't see anything. I started to take off one of my new golf shoes to step in the water and find my cart and golf bag. Roger said, "I wouldn't do that if I were you."

"Why not? I've got to get my bag!"

"Might be snakes in there. I wouldn't chance it."

"Snakes?" I thought. *"There ain't no way in the world a snake could live in this dirty, filthy water."* But, why take the chance? I can always wash my new shoes when I get home . . . they'll be fine. So, I stepped in the water; except it was more mud than water. My foot slid down the side and didn't stop until I was in crap over my knee. But I did feel my cart in the water. I reached down to pull it up but it wouldn't budge. It was snagged on a submerged root in the water.

I had to put my other foot in the swampy water, which also had a new golf shoe on it, and struggled and strained to try to free my cart and bag from the roots. I finally got it free but it was so waterlogged and heavy that I couldn't pick it up with my feet sliding in the mud. Good old Roger reached down from the safety of the bank and helped me haul my once new cart and bag and phone and towel up out of the mire. It was not pretty.

My once new golf shoes looked like something from the throw-away bin at Goodwill. Since I was in water up to mid-thigh level, my once new shorts were ruined. My poor golf bag set on the bank oozing mud and water from every crevice. My once new golf cart looked as though it came from Fred Sanford's junkyard.

My wallet was ruined, my phone didn't work any longer, and my medicine had totally dissolved. I unzipped all the pouches to let as much water out as I could. I turned the golf bag upside down and dumped out the water and my clubs onto the ground. I felt as though my most faithful and loving dog had just died . . . and I don't even own a dog.

I finally put all my soaked golf clubs back in the bag and pulled the entire mess back away from the creek. Then, I heard Roger say, "Well, you about ready? Looks like you've got about 140 yards left to the green."

I didn't finish the hole and conceded a double-bogey as I left a trail of murky, dirty, brown, wastewater down the cart path all the way to the next tee. And people still ask me why I don't like this hole!

***

But . . . now that I've had nearly a year to think about these events, I understand that it wasn't the hole's fault. It wasn't Roger's fault (maybe). It wasn't the creek's fault, or the hill's fault, or even my fault—sometimes things happen which are simply out of your control. Should I have put the brake on my cart when I briefly stopped? Yes. Could my cart roll down that hill again and slip through that tiny opening like it did that

97

fateful day? No way, impossible. But it happened. Just like things similar to this have happened in your life, and will continue to happen. That's what life is. It's not scripted, things happen which you have no control over. You somehow have to recover and move on--pick up the pieces, dry everything off, and slosh onwards toward the next objective. It isn't easy.

When I arrived on the next tee, my shoes and socks were squishy. The grips on my golf clubs were soaked—I wasn't sure if I could even hold onto the club as I swung it. Water was still dripping from my bag and my iPhone was making all sorts of weird noises. But guess what? I parred the final two holes.

So can you!

#17

This is a long par 3 hole with a small creek in front and sand traps to the left and right. After the previous hole, you don't really care what it looks like; you're just happy to be here. Most of the time, after I've bogeyed or double-bogeyed #16, when I arrive on this tee, I'm still mad. One day, my playing partner, let's call him Jack, saw that my temper had not yet abated, so he felt he had to say something to get my mind off the previous devilish hole.

He said, "I read on the internet this morning that there is a new study about women and how they feel about their asses. The results were very interesting:

10% of women think their ass is too skinny.

30% of women think their ass is too fat.

60% say they don't care. They love him anyway. He is a good man and they wouldn't trade him for the world."

Thanks, Jack, I needed that, and even though I still missed the green, I felt better.

Gary Hope

***

Your round of golf is getting near the end. Sometimes, if you've been walking the course, you're tired and ready for a cold drink. Or, if you've been playing well, you're ready to keep going. Or, maybe the friendship and companionship with your friends are more important than any score you may have. Similar to your life and how aging affects us all. I've known people who have had so many health issues and personal setbacks, that by the 17th hole of their life they're ready for it to end. It's sad.

I'll always remember my stepfather, Bob, a great and wonderful man who loved golf and life. But after his wife died, who was my mother, he lost his joy for life. He started having health issues until it finally resulted in his last hospital stay, which wasn't good. The last time I saw him, he could barely open his eyes, but when he did and saw me, he said, "Gar, I'm ready to go. I'm ready."

I understand how he felt. It wasn't easy and I didn't want him to give up . . . but I understood. Health issues, personal setbacks, family crises, financial horrors, and broken hearts can affect us all in negative and dangerous ways. However, just the opposite can also happen! You're playing well, making pars, and even throwing in a birdie or two—golf is fun! You don't want it to end . . . in fact, after #18, you say, "Let's play nine more!" Yes . . . very groovy.

The walk from the 17th tee to the 17th green is all downhill. It's almost too easy. And this green is the only green on the back nine that doesn't have hills and contours on it—it's pretty tame and easy to read. I like this hole; even though it's a bit long for us old guys, it's pretty fair and gives you a good chance for par. Reminds me a little of contemplating retirement. Once you make that decision, it all seems downhill afterward. No more deadlines, no more headaches, no more sucking up to bosses and directors and presidents . . . just reeeelax.

The only problem with this 17th hole is that to reach the 18th tee you must walk up a steep hill, which after walking seventeen other holes, is not very much fun. But you know that it's the last hole and drinks are waiting at the clubhouse. Those thoughts make the journey a little easier. Reminds me of the thoughts you have when retiring from work. If you've saved properly and Social Security is still around (who knows what's going to happen with that) and you've made some timely investments, then hey, you're feeling good. The future looks bright and life seems rosy . . . for most people.

***

I was walking up this steep hill to the 18th tee last year with a fellow I met on the course that day—I had never seen him before. He was a pretty good golfer and an even better human being . . . and he was an ex-Catholic priest. I liked playing with him that day and enjoyed talking with him even more. He had insightful messages and interesting outlooks on life. Even though he limited my vocabulary on certain bad shots, it was all worth it to listen to him talk and describe some of his experiences.

I remember walking up this hill from 17 to 18 and he told me something funny that helped with the pain of pushing my cart up that incline. He said he was talking to a group of young kids one day about vestments and he asked them, "Why do you think I wear this collar?"

One kid answered, "Because it kills ticks and fleas up to 30 days?"

I laughed all the way up to the 18th tee. I'm not sure why, but when we arrived at the tee area, he took a deep breath and stared up at the sky, as if he was looking at something. I looked up as well to see if there was an airplane up there, or maybe a buzzard or hawk soaring by—but I didn't see anything. Then he pulled his driver from his golf bag, looked over at me, and said, "Gary, how cool is it that the same God who created mountains and oceans and galaxies looked at you, or me, and thought the world needed one of us, too."

#18

The Last Hole

Well, we've made it safely up the steep hill from the green on 17 to the tee here at 18 . . . that's saying something! Some of us just thank the Lord we're still alive and breathing, while others may be thinking of calling the grill to place an order that will be ready when we finish. And, we have an excellent grill and bar area, with extremely efficient, talented, handsome, and beautiful staff members. Of course, Shirley is smarter, harder-working, and more beautiful than all the rest, but Bing and Kay and Kelsey come in a close second. I shouldn't say that . . . they're all great and will do whatever they can to make your visit wonderful.

Anyway, back to golf. This last finishing hole is very pleasant and a great relief after the previous grueling holes. It's a par 5 that is FLAT! Can you believe it? The left side of the fairway is lined with trees and thick undergrowth and there are some trees on the right side as well . . . but it's FLAT. There are bunkers on the left and right sides of the green, but who cares? You didn't have to walk up any hills to get here. Making a birdie on this hole is always a possibility if you hit two or three good shots. And, let me tell you, making a birdie on the last hole of the day is always great.

I've found in the past that after you tee off and start down the fairway of this last, flat hole, that my playing partners are always feeling good. No more hills to climb, hopefully, no more bogeys, maybe even the possibility of a birdie, and the clubhouse is just up ahead with cold beverages, sandwiches, and more cold beverages. Everyone is feeling good. Because of this euphoria, I've heard some half-way funny stories as we walked this last fairway. Like this one from my buddy, Mike:

An 85-year-old man goes to see his doctor for his regular physical exam. The doctor says that the man needs to provide a sperm sample and gives him a jar saying, "Take this jar home with you and come back tomorrow with a sperm sample."

The next day the old man goes back to the doctor and gives him the jar, which is as clean and empty as when the doctor gave it to him.

So the doctor asks what happened and why there is no sperm sample in the jar. The old man says, "Well, doc, it's like this. I tried first with my right hand, but nothing. Then I tried with my left hand, but still nothing. Then I asked my wife for help. She tried with her right hand--nothing; then with her left--still nothing. She tried with her mouth, first with the teeth in, then with her teeth out--still nothing. We even called up Maisie, the lady next door and she tried, too, first with both hands, then an armpit, and she even tried squeezing it between her knees, but still nothing."

The doctor is really shocked by all this and asks incredulously, "You asked your neighbor???"

The old man replies, "Yep, not one of us could get the jar open."

***

Then, you have other friends who are more, let's say, scholarly. I was walking down this last fairway one day with Randy, and he suddenly said, "Gary, did you know that one time in China, 830,000 people died in one day due to an earthquake."

"No, Randy, I didn't know that."

He looked over at me and said, "Yep, it's true; you can look it up."

That was very interesting, but I liked Mike's story better. The point is, we all see things differently. We all react to things differently. And, on this last hole, similar to life, when we're on the backstretch, it makes us think in ways we didn't think earlier in our lives. Sometimes, on the backend of our lives, we're happy and feel good about how things have turned out. Other times, there may be things we wish we'd done differently: been a better husband or wife; been a better dad; invested sooner and more wisely; finished your education; changed jobs for one with a better opportunity; traveled more; done more; etc., etc., etc.

This backstretch gives us all ample time to rethink things we've done and dream of things we wished we would've done. It can be a time filled with good memories, or a time filled with regrets . . . it's all up to you. Don't dwell too much; none of us is perfect. We all wish we'd done some things differently than others. Don't beat yourself up. I could fill up the next ten pages with things I wish I'd done differently, but what good would it do?

Enjoy this last FLAT fairway. Try your best to birdie this hole. Don't dwell on the ball you hit in the lake at #15, or the ball you sliced in the creek at #4, or the green you four-putted on #7, or the 830,000 Chinese who died in an earthquake. Let that stuff go! This is the only life you're going to have. Enjoy it! Keep trudging the hills and woods and creeks at this beautiful course and be thankful for all the friends you have here and the family you have at home. Trust me . . . we are blessed to be able to be here.

Thanks, Lynn, Shannon, Shirley, staff, grounds crew, and all the others who make this such a pleasurable place to visit.

***

Now, as I'm sitting in one of the rocking chairs at the clubhouse after my round, enjoying a cold beverage, I'm reminded of one last humorous story:

One day a Scottssman, who has been stranded on a desert island for over ten long years, sees an unusual speck on the horizon.

"It's certainly not a ship," he thinks to himself. As the speck gets closer and closer, he begins to rule out the possibilities of a small boat, then even a raft. Suddenly, emerging from the surf comes a drop dead gorgeous blonde woman wearing a wetsuit and scuba gear. She approaches the stunned man and says to him, "Tell me, how long has it been since you've had a cigarette?"

"Ten years," replies the Scottsman. With that, she reaches over and unzips a waterproof pocket on her left sleeve and pulls out a pack of fresh cigarettes. He takes one, lights it, takes a long drag and says, "Faith and begorah! Is that good!"

"And how long has it been since you've had a sip of good Scotch Whiskey?" she asks him.

Trembling, the castaway replies, "Ten years." She reaches over, unzips her right sleeve, pulls out a flask and hands it to him.

He opens the flask, takes a long swig and says, "Tis absolutely fantastic!"

At this point she starts slowly unzipping the long zipper that runs down the front of her wet suit, looks at the man and asks, "And how long has it been since you've played around?"

With tears in his eyes, the Scott falls to his knees and sobs, "Oh, Sweet Jesus! Don't tell me you've got golf clubs in there too."

***

And, finally, thanks Uncle Paul for introducing me to this frustrating, bewildering, perplexing, flabbergasting, puzzling, mystifying, thrilling, and pleasurable game we love. But most of all, thanks for being my Uncle Paul.

As usual, Mr. Larry McRacken has edited this book for me and done an outstanding job.

Thanks, Lance

And, Mr. Dickie Nye has provided useful information and facts which I have used.

Thanks, Susan, for all you have done and all that you continue to do.

And if you are interested, here are several of my other novels:

It's Too Late to Die Young Now
Abbey
The Girl From Tir-na-nOg
The Confluence
Friends
Niamh
Ana
Allen & Bill
Noah

www.ingramcontent.com/pod-product-compliance
Lightning Source LLC
Chambersburg PA
CBHW071956070426
42453CB00008BA/829